Coping with

CROHN'S DISEASE AND ULCERATIVE COLITIS

Christina Potter

The Rosen Publishing Group, Inc.
New York

For Dan and Gina

Published in 2004 by The Rosen Publishing Group, Inc.
29 East 21st Street, New York, NY 10010

First Edition

Library of Congress Cataloging-in-Publication Data

Potter, Christina.
Coping with Crohn's disease and ulcerative colitis/
Christina Potter.
  v. cm.—(Coping)
Includes bibliographical references and index.
Contents: Inflammatory bowel disease: some facts—Tests for IBD—Medical treatments—Surgery—Diet and nutrition —Emotional aspects—Tips for daily life.
ISBN 0-8239-3962-6
1. Inflammatory bowel diseases—Juvenile literature.
[1. Inflammatory bowel diseases. 2. Crohn's disease.
3. Diseases.]
I. Title. II. Series.

RC862.I53P68 2003
616.3'44—dc21

                                                2003000253

Manufactured in the United States of America

Contents

Introduction

When Darcy was ten years old, she was active in school and played on a traveling soccer team. She seemed perfectly healthy.

Then she started getting bad stomachaches.

"At first," she says, "my doctor told me I had something like migraines, only in my stomach. Then he said maybe I was constipated. But they never took any tests."

Her stomach pain grew worse, and she started missing school, but her doctor still couldn't tell her what was wrong. Finally, her parents took her to see a gastroenterologist, a doctor who specializes in the digestive system. This doctor suggested she might be lactose-intolerant.

"The gastroenterologist never did any tests, either," says Darcy. "Never took any blood work. I remember at one point, he actually said to my mother, 'The child looks well . . . she is well.' But people can look well. You have no idea how sick they really are."

After another doctor told her that she might have celiac disease, a condition in which people cannot tolerate gluten, she was referred to a pediatric gastroenterologist. This doctor performed a colonoscopy to view the inside of Darcy's intestines.

"I remember waking up after the colonoscopy, and my mom and dad were just looking at me and saying how proud they were," she says. "I had so much inflammation all over my intestines, and bleeding ulcers, that the doctor said most adults would have collapsed and gone into the ER weeks ago."

After a year of trying to find out what was wrong, Darcy finally had an answer. She had Crohn's disease, which is a type of inflammatory bowel disease, or IBD. Her doctor explained that Crohn's causes inflammation, or swelling, in the intestines. This inflammation, and the accompanying ulcers, was responsible for her pain.

Crohn's disease, a chronic illness, cannot be cured. It may go away for long periods of time, but there is always the chance that it will come back. "I really didn't know anything about Crohn's when I was diagnosed," Darcy says. "I was actually relieved at first, because it wasn't celiac disease, and I thought now I could eat whatever I wanted."

Because the disease in her intestines was so wide-spread, surgery to remove the inflamed areas was out of the question. She began intensive therapy on prednisone, an anti-inflammatory medication that helps treat Crohn's disease and another form of IBD called ulcerative colitis.

The medications helped relieve her pain and started to heal the damage of Crohn's disease. But they also drastically changed the way she looked and weakened her bones. "I got so much better with the prednisone," she says. "But I got almost every known side effect. I broke two small bones, so I had to stop playing soccer. I wanted to eat everything. I gained sixty pounds over seven months. And my face—my doctor said she'd never seen anyone so swollen before."

The fact that she had a chronic illness, along with the pain, exhaustion, and physical changes, started to take its toll. Darcy became seriously depressed. "That first year, I literally did not want to be seen," she says. "I hid out in my house. I went on the homebound program and lost most of my friends. I hated how I looked. I thought I was a freak with a disease."

Her attitude toward Crohn's disease changed when she attended a camp for kids with IBD. For the first time, she met other people dealing with the same kinds of things. "One night, I ended up pouring out my heart to the executive director, and it really changed my life. It made me see that I can live with this."

Darcy returned to middle school and found that her teachers were sympathetic once they understood her situation. She started to feel better physically and also felt more in control of her life. With time, she discovered ways to deal with the daily challenges of IBD. "Sometimes, you just have to get through the day . . . and then move on. Because it's going to get better."

Because it had helped her so much to talk to someone who understood what she was going through, Darcy decided she wanted to help other people. Now seventeen, she is a peer counselor for young people with IBD and is involved in the Crohn's and Colitis Foundation of America. She started college a year ahead of schedule and plans to pursue a career in medicine.

For her, she says, a positive attitude has made all the difference. "I would never want to be known as the poor child who's sick," she says. "I tell people I have Crohn's, but I don't want them to feel sorry for me. I'm a strong believer in having a positive frame of mind."

Most people have never heard of inflammatory bowel disease. But if you are suffering from Crohn's disease or ulcerative colitis, you are not alone. Approximately one million people in the United States have a form of IBD; about 200,000 of these are younger than eighteen.

Inflammatory bowel disease is not always easy to live with. It is a painful condition that requires medical attention and can result in hospitalizations and surgery. It can also be emotionally difficult to accept. But most people find that after some initial adjustments, they are able to adapt quite well to life with Crohn's disease or ulcerative colitis.

This book discusses the characteristics of IBD and ways of managing the disease through medications, surgery, and diet. It also talks about emotional responses to Crohn's and colitis and gives suggestions for dealing with daily challenges. Many of these suggestions come from young people who are themselves living with IBD.

Taking some time to acquaint yourself with the facts of IBD and learning ways to cope positively with it are two of the best things you can do for your health. Like Darcy, you will probably find that having Crohn's disease or ulcerative colitis is not as frightening or as hard to manage as it may once have seemed.

Inflammatory Bowel Disease: Some Facts

Inflammatory bowel disease (IBD) is a general term used to describe Crohn's disease and ulcerative colitis. Both Crohn's and colitis are diseases of the digestive tract, sharing many of the same characteristics and symptoms. In fact, they are so similar that doctors often have trouble telling them apart. If it isn't clear which type of IBD you have, your doctor may simply tell you that you have a form of inflammatory bowel disease, or indeterminate colitis.

Although many people get them confused, IBD is not the same as irritable bowel syndrome, or IBS. IBS is a bowel disorder that causes many of the same symptoms as Crohn's disease and ulcerative colitis. It is generally a less serious condition, however, that does not require prompt medical attention and rarely leads to hospitalization or surgery.

An estimated one million people in the United States suffer from Crohn's disease and ulcerative colitis. Most find out they have IBD as adolescents or young adults, although it is not unusual for someone to develop the disease either earlier or later in life. Children as young as a few months old can have IBD.

IBD is a chronic disease, which means it will not go away. But most people with Crohn's or colitis are not sick all the time. They go through cycles of flare-ups, when the disease is active, and remissions, when symptoms disappear. When IBD does flare up, it usually requires some sort of treatment before going back into remission.

Living with IBD can be a challenge. It is a frustrating, painful, and sometimes embarrassing disease that may require periodic hospitalizations and lifestyle changes. But most people find it is something they eventually get used to. "You learn to deal with it," says Dan, who is thirty. "I've had Crohn's for ten years now, and it really hasn't stopped me from doing the things I love to do. It can be a deterrent sometimes, but those times are relatively rare."

Crohn's Disease

Crohn's disease is named for Dr. Burrill B. Crohn, who identified the disease in 1932. It is a chronic illness that can be treated with medication, diet, and surgery, but at this time there is no cure.

With Crohn's disease, the walls of the intestines become inflamed, making them swollen and painful. The inflammation can cause damage to all layers of intestinal tissue and often leads to ulcerations (sores), scarring, and other complications. It may also thicken the intestinal walls so much that the bowel channel becomes too narrow for contents to pass through.

Although Crohn's can affect any part of the digestive tract, from the esophagus to the anus, it is most common in the ileum (end of the small intestine) and the colon (large intestine). The diseased areas usually appear in patches, separated by segments of healthy intestine.

Depending on which part of your intestinal tract is affected, your doctor may refer to your condition as ileitis, which is inflammation in the ileum; ileocolitis, or inflammation in the ileum and the colon; or Crohn's colitis, which is inflammation in the colon. Because the location of the disease influences the type of symptoms you experience and often affects treatment of these symptoms, it can be helpful to know which type of Crohn's disease you have.

Most people experience periods of flare-ups followed by periods of remission. Flare-ups vary in severity from person to person. Some cases respond quickly to medication and go into remission after just a week or two. Other people have more difficulty achieving remission and may require hospitalization or surgery before symptoms disappear.

Remissions, like flare-ups, are unpredictable. They can last a few months or many years. The length of a remission may depend on many factors, including the severity and location of disease, and the form of treatment you are using. Through trial and error, many people eventually find the treatment that is most effective for them and are able to stay in remission for longer periods of time.

Ulcerative Colitis

Like Crohn's disease, ulcerative colitis causes inflammation of the intestinal tract and many of the accompanying problems. However, ulcerative colitis appears exclusively in the colon and the rectum, and affects only the innermost lining of the intestinal wall. It appears in continuous stretches, whereas Crohn's usually shows up in patches.

Depending on the exact location and extent of the disease, your doctor may refer to your condition by one of several names. Ulcerative colitis of the rectum is called ulcerative proctitis. Ulcerative proctitis generally stays solely in the rectum and does not spread to the colon. Other forms of ulcerative colitis are proctosigmoiditis, or inflammation in the rectum and lower part of the colon, and pan-ulcerative, or total colitis, which causes inflammation throughout the entire colon. When inflammation appears in larger stretches of the colon, pain and other symptoms can be more severe.

Like Crohn's disease, ulcerative colitis goes through cycles of flare-ups and remission. Occasionally, remission happens naturally, but in most cases it is the result of medical treatment. In severe cases, when ulcerative colitis does not respond to medication or poses an emergency threat, the entire colon and rectum may be surgically removed (see chapter 4). Because it eliminates the source of the disease, this surgery is a cure for ulcerative colitis.

What Causes IBD?

No one knows for sure what causes Crohn's disease and ulcerative colitis. Researchers suspect that it may be triggered by a complex combination of genetics, immune response, and environmental factors. While it is true that emotional stress and certain foods may aggravate IBD, these things do not cause the disease itself.

According to the Crohn's and Colitis Foundation of America (CCFA), roughly 20 percent of Crohn's and colitis patients have a close relative with IBD. But it is not yet clear what role genetics plays in transmitting the disease.

The intestinal inflammation seen in IBD seems to be the result of an overactive immune response. When a foreign substance enters the intestinal lining, the body overreacts, causing an unusual amount of inflammation that does not go away once the threat has been eliminated. What isn't clear is why the body responds in this way, or if there is a specific environmental trigger that causes this reaction.

Investigation into the causes of IBD is receiving more attention and funding as people become aware of the disease and the problems it causes. National associations such as the CCFA and the National Institutes of Health (NIH) are funding research efforts in an attempt to isolate a cause and, hopefully, a cure.

Who Gets IBD?

IBD occurs almost exclusively in developed nations and rarely appears in Africa, South America, or most parts of Asia. In developed countries, however, it seems to affect all ethnic groups, although it is most common among Caucasians. People of Jewish descent living in Europe, North America, and Israel have roughly a five times higher risk of developing IBD than the general population.

Although researchers suspect that environment may somehow play a role in the onset of IBD, there is currently no strong evidence linking any one environmental factor to either Crohn's disease or ulcerative colitis. Some studies have indicated a connection between IBD and smoking, but since many non-smokers also develop Crohn's and colitis, this is not fully understood.

Symptoms of IBD

Each person experiences IBD a little differently. It is rare to find two people who have exactly the same symptoms during a flare-up. But almost everyone with Crohn's disease or ulcerative colitis suffers from some of the following symptoms:

- Diarrhea

- Abdominal cramping and pain

- Fever

- Fatigue

- Appetite loss

- Weight loss

- Joint pain

- Nausea

- Rectal bleeding

Ulcerative colitis usually starts with bloody diarrhea that gets worse over time. People with ulcerative colitis may also feel like they constantly need to have a bowel movement. Although the discomfort and cramping might go away after using the bathroom, they usually reappear shortly after.

Dustin, sixteen, has had ulcerative colitis since he was seven years old, and he has learned to recognize early signs of a flare-up. "When I start to get sick," he says, "I get really tired and my left side cramps up. If I move, it kills me."

Jessica is thirteen and has had ulcerative colitis almost all her life. She was diagnosed at three months old. She describes her usual symptoms as "cramping, stomach pain, loose bowel movements, mouth ulcers, and joint pains."

Early signs of Crohn's disease are abdominal cramping (mostly after meals) and frequent diarrhea. "I get especially crampy before and after bowel movements," says Dan. "And I used to get very loose stools. Food would go rushing through me, so I'd have to go to the bathroom a lot, and it was uncomfortable when I did. There would be days when I had to run to the bathroom every ten minutes."

Symptoms vary greatly in severity from person to person. Some people experience only minor discomfort and are able to manage the disease with medication or diet or both. Other people suffer more serious pain and complications that can lead to hospitalization or surgery.

Complications

Complications arising from IBD fall into two categories: "local," meaning that they occur in the digestive tract, where IBD is present, and "systemic" or "extraintestinal," meaning that they affect other parts of the body.

Some of these complications show up in both types of IBD, and others are specific to either Crohn's disease or ulcerative colitis.

Strictures and Obstructions

A stricture is a narrowed segment of intestine, usually caused by scarring from inflamed tissue. Strictures are found only in Crohn's disease and are most common in the small intestine. They may appear during flare-ups or shortly after a flare-up, when the inflamed tissue is starting to heal. To positively identify a stricture, your doctor will need to perform an X ray or an endoscopy (see chapter 2).

Strictures do not usually pose any additional problems. If they occur during a flare-up, they may be treated with medication that will help reduce inflammation. In severe cases, however, the intestine becomes so narrow that contents cannot pass through at all. When this happens, it is called obstruction or blockage.

Obstruction is serious and painful, and should be treated quickly. To get rid of the stricture, your doctor may surgically remove part of your intestine or perform an operation called a strictureplasty (see chapter 4).

Fistulas and Abscesses

In some cases of Crohn's disease, inflammation may result in fistulas, which are abnormal channels leading from one section of the intestine to another. Fistulas may also form between the intestine and another organ, such as the bladder, vagina, or skin. They occur when the intestine grows so thick from inflammation that it gets too close to another organ, and a small passage opens to connect the two.

Many people are able to live with fistulas for a long time without experiencing problems or pain. Because of this, and because they are only visible by X ray or endoscopy, it is possible to have a fistula for some time without knowing it. Once they are discovered, small fistulas may respond to medication; others are more stubborn or serious and may require surgery.

Sometimes, a fistula will become infected, causing a pocket of pus, or abscess, to form. An abscess will cause pain and fever, and must be surgically drained.

Perforation of the Bowel

Although relatively rare, perforation can occur in either Crohn's disease or ulcerative colitis. If the intestine becomes sufficiently weakened, it may tear open, creating a hole, or perforation. Intestinal contents can then escape through this hole and into the abdominal cavity. Bowel perforation can cause fever, nausea, abdominal pain, and vomiting. It is a serious condition that usually requires emergency surgery.

Toxic Megacolon

Seen almost exclusively in ulcerative colitis, this potentially life-threatening condition is very rare. It occurs when the colon becomes so inflamed and weak that it is in danger of rupturing. Toxic megacolon causes fever, abdominal pain and distention, and possibly shock. If the inflammation cannot be controlled through medicines, it becomes necessary to remove the colon surgically.

Systemic Complications

Although no one is entirely sure why these conditions occur, or why they affect only some people with IBD, most systemic complications seem to be related to failures in the immune system or to nutritional problems resulting from IBD. Medications used to treat IBD may also be responsible in some cases.

Not everyone with IBD will develop systemic complications. Since early detection makes treatment easier, it is a good idea to be aware of the following potential problems:

➶ Arthritis

➶ Osteoporosis

➶ Skin conditions

➶ Liver disease

➶ Inflammation of the eye

➶ Anemia

➶ Malnutrition and growth problems

➶ Kidney stones

Roughly 20 percent of people with IBD have problems with arthritis, usually in their ankles, knees, elbows, and wrists. Pain generally appears along with other symptoms during a flare-up and goes away when IBD goes into remission. Monique, age fourteen, has problems with her joints during flare-ups. "I get really tired, and my joints hurt," she says. "That's actually the first sign that I'm getting sick. My knees and my ankles and my fingers start to ache."

Other complications may occur in association with joint pain or appear on their own. If you notice red, bumpy patches on your skin, pain in your eyes, or sores in your mouth, especially during a flare-up, you should see your doctor. Although many problems will improve on their own when IBD enters remission, it is important to get a medical evaluation. Problems with the eye, in particular, require prompt attention.

Osteoporosis is a special risk for people who have used corticosteroid medications (see chapter 3) for long periods of time. These drugs contribute to bone loss, which is already a problem for people with IBD. If you are taking corticosteroids to treat Crohn's disease or ulcerative colitis, or if you have a lot of disease in your small intestine (which can cause poor calcium absorption), your doctor may want you to have periodic bone density tests to check for problems.

Growth problems are a fact of life for many young people with IBD. If you have trouble eating enough food, or absorbing the food you do eat, you may not grow as quickly as most kids your age. To add to the problem, corticosteroid treatment (common for IBD) can also result in delayed growth. Usually, however, once you get your IBD under control and restore a proper nutritional balance, growth will resume as normal.

IBD and Cancer

People with IBD have a slightly higher chance of developing colon cancer than the general population. But this does not necessarily mean that you are at high risk; only about 5 to 10 percent of people with IBD actually do develop cancer.

Those most at risk are people who have suffered from widespread ulcerative colitis (involving a large area of the colon) for more than eight to ten years. Recent studies have suggested that people with Crohn's disease also have an increased risk of cancer, but this connection has not been as extensively studied. On average, IBD patients with colon cancer are between forty and fifty years old.

Most doctors will want to check regularly for signs of cancer in people who are at increased risk. This means that, once you reach a certain age, you might have to have a colonoscopy and biopsies every year or two. Biopsies are painless procedures, in which the doctor removes small tissue samples from your intestines and examines them more closely under a microscope. If your doctor finds dysplasia (abnormal cells that might be pre-cancerous) or evidence of actual cancer, there is a chance that you will need surgery.

Cancer is a frightening prospect. But even if you are among the small percentage of people with IBD who do develop colon cancer, it is likely that you will be able to treat it effectively. Because IBD patients are screened regularly, your chances of discovering cancer early are very good.

Getting Diagnosed

Few people walk into their doctor's office complaining of diarrhea, cramping, and weight loss and come out that same day with a diagnosis of IBD. Unfortunately, the "tell-tale" symptoms of Crohn's disease and ulcerative colitis are characteristic of a lot of other conditions, so many doctors do not immediately suspect IBD. Usually, the diagnosis comes from a specialist in digestive medicine, called a gastroenterologist.

It is not at all uncommon for doctors to initially tell people that they have another illness. Coby, who is seventeen, went back to her doctor several times before she got a correct diagnosis. "At first the doctor thought I had giardiasis, because I was getting bad stomach cramps," she said. "But those tests came back clear. Then the pain moved to my lower right side and I thought it was appendicitis." Two days later, she was hospitalized for an appendectomy, because a CT scan showed that an abscess on her appendix had ruptured and leaked. The abscess, doctors later discovered, was caused by Crohn's disease.

Since Crohn's disease and ulcerative colitis share many of the same symptoms, it is sometimes hard for doctors to distinguish between the two. Monique has been sick for more than five years and still doesn't know which type of IBD she has. "First they told me I had colitis," says Monique. "And now they're not quite sure if it's colitis or Crohn's."

Getting diagnosed with Crohn's disease or ulcerative colitis can be a lengthy, emotional process, lasting months or even years. Once your doctor suspects IBD, it is still necessary to undergo tests to pinpoint the disease. Then, when the diagnosis finally comes, it can be a mixed blessing. On the one hand, you may feel relieved to understand what has been making you sick. On the other hand, the prospect of living with a chronic illness is upsetting.

"I was diagnosed with Crohn's when I was twenty-one," says Dan. "But I went through about a year of misdiagnoses.

I was told that I had stress, stress-related ulcers, indigestion, lactose intolerance, burst appendix, and food poisoning. I was so frustrated about being misdiagnosed that when they said I had Crohn's, there was some validation in it. I thought, OK, I have Crohn's disease. It wasn't for a few months that it really sunk in."

The good news is that when you get a proper diagnosis you can start to learn about the disease and begin to treat it. Gathering as much information as possible will help you stay in control of your situation and your health. You may also find that the more you know about IBD, the easier it is for you to live with it.

Tests for IBD

Because IBD is an internal disease, the only way your doctor can really understand what's happening in your body is by looking inside. This means that even after you've been diagnosed, you will probably need periodic tests to see how your condition is progressing.

If the prospect of being pricked, prodded, and probed makes you uneasy, you are not alone. Fortunately, however, most people agree that the tests for IBD are not as bad as they sound. "You get used to them," says Dan. "I used to be more self-conscious about some of the procedures, but now it's really not a big deal."

Understanding as much as possible about the tests, and recognizing that they are a crucial part of managing your condition, can help alleviate your fears as well. "If you know what's going to happen, you're not as freaked out," says Monique.

Remember that as stressful as they may be, tests help you take control of your life. They give you and your doctors more information about your medical condition, making it easier to treat the IBD. "The attitude that I have is, once I get through this test, they're going to be able to tell how to fix me," says Darcy. "These tests are to make me feel better, so it's OK if they're a little uncomfortable for a while."

Here are some of the more common procedures used in diagnosing and monitoring IBD. You may never have to have some of these tests, but if you do, it can be helpful to know how and why they are performed.

Blood Tests

Blood testing is one of the first steps in diagnosing IBD. The results will not determine for certain whether or not you have IBD, but they can hint at the presence of Crohn's disease or ulcerative colitis and also rule out other possibilities.

A blood count can also help your doctor determine how much inflammation is present during a flare-up, or how well you are responding to a particular medication. Because of this, you will probably need to have regular blood tests even after you know for sure that you have IBD. Usually, your doctor will need to collect a few vials of blood, and the process involves just a needle prick.

Unless you are nervous about needles, blood testing will probably not be an ordeal. If you dread the process, it may be helpful to look away while the blood is being drawn. Darcy, who doesn't like needles, says she has found another thing that helps her get through the process. "People always think this is funny," she says, "but I hold my mom's hand, and it does help . . . even at age seventeen."

Stool Tests

Stool tests are another diagnostic tool. They are extremely helpful for ruling out other conditions that mimic IBD. Before doing more invasive testing, your doctor will most likely collect a stool sample to make sure your symptoms are not caused by a bacterial infection or parasite. The results of the test will confirm or rule out the existence of salmonella, shigella, giardia, and other organisms that can cause symptoms similar to those of IBD.

Barium X Rays

X rays are one of the most common tools for diagnosing Crohn's disease and ulcerative colitis. They are also helpful for distinguishing between the two types of IBD and for monitoring the severity and location of inflammation. Because of this, you may need to have occasional X rays so that your doctor can check for changes in your condition.

In order for your digestive tract to show up in X rays, it must be highlighted with a substance called barium. Barium is a material that coats the lining of the digestive tract, making it appear bright white on the X rays. If you are getting an upper GI (gastrointestinal), you will take the barium by mouth. If you are getting a lower GI, the doctor will introduce the barium through your rectum.

Upper GI

Your doctor performs an upper GI series to examine your esophagus, stomach, and the beginning of your small intestine. The X rays will help identify any inflammation, blockages, or other abnormalities in the digestive tract. The upper GI is used for identifying and monitoring Crohn's disease, because colitis appears only in the lower digestive tract.

Your stomach will need to be empty for the procedure, so you will not be able to eat anything for several hours before the test. You should not smoke or chew gum before the tests because these activities can trigger stomach secretions that may interfere with the quality of the X rays. Your doctor will give you other detailed instructions before the procedure.

When you arrive for the test, you will drink barium, in a thick, milkshake-like fluid. The barium has a chalky taste and is sometimes flavored with strawberry or chocolate. In addition to the barium, you may be asked to swallow baking soda crystals. These crystals help create gas in your stomach. While the gas may be a little uncomfortable (making you feel the need to burp), it is best to keep the gas in your stomach if possible because gas makes the X rays clearer.

The doctor will use a machine called a fluoroscope to watch the barium's progress through your digestive tract. Once it has lined the upper gastrointestinal tract, the doctor will start taking X rays. Unless you are lying on an automatic table that allows the doctor to tilt you into different positions, you will be asked to shift position periodically so that the barium fully coats all necessary areas of the digestive tract.

The procedure is not painful and usually lasts about thirty to forty-five minutes, depending on the areas that your doctor wants to view. Afterward, you may have stools that are colored white or gray for a few days because of the barium.

Most patients find that the upper GI is not an unpleasant test. "It's actually kind of fun," says Dan, who has had numerous X rays. "It's not painful, and you get to watch the barium going down your esophagus and into your stomach. It's interesting to see what's going on inside of you."

Barium Enema

This test is similar to an upper GI but gives your doctor a view of the lower portion of your digestive tract. It can help identify inflammation of the intestine's inner lining, which appears in ulcerative colitis. It can also detect the presence of fistulas in Crohn's disease.

Your doctor will give you detailed instructions about how to prepare for the test. These will probably include being on a liquid diet and drinking a bowel prep, which helps to empty your digestive tract.

To coat your lower bowel with barium, the doctor will insert an enema tube into your rectum. While this may not sound pleasant, it is probably less uncomfortable than some of the daily symptoms you are already experiencing. A lower GI may cause some cramping and the urge to defecate, but since these are common symptoms of IBD, you will probably have a higher tolerance for them than most people. Keep in mind that the cramping sensation should ease in about a minute.

Once the barium is inside, the doctor will use a fluoroscope to watch it move through your intestines. You will probably have to change positions several times to ensure that the barium coats all necessary parts of your bowel. Then, your doctor will take X rays. If you are having a double, or air-contrast, study, your doctor will let a small amount of air into your colon before taking more X rays.

After the test, you will go to the bathroom to get rid of the barium left in your bowel. Your stools will probably be a whitish gray color for a couple of days, but other than that, you should not experience anything unusual once the test is complete.

Endoscopy

An endoscopy is a procedure that allows your doctor to view the inside of the gastrointestinal tract, using a long, thin, flexible tube called an endoscope. The doctor carefully guides the endoscope through the digestive channel, while a camera on the end of the scope sends pictures back to a monitor. The images can help diagnose IBD, determine the location of the disease, and identify complications of either Crohn's disease or ulcerative colitis.

To examine your esophagus, stomach, and the beginning of your small intestine, your doctor will perform an upper GI endoscopy. To look at the lower portion of the digestive tract, he or she will do either a sigmoidoscopy or colonoscopy. Endoscopies are considered safe procedures, and because you will be sedated, you should not feel much during the tests themselves.

Upper GI Endoscopy

This test gives a clear view of your upper gastrointestinal tract and can help your doctor identify complications that do not show up well on X rays. It takes between fifteen and thirty minutes to complete.

You are usually not able to eat anything for eight to ten hours before the test because anything sitting in your stomach can block the view of the endoscope. When you arrive at the doctor's, you will receive a sedative. This will help you relax but will not put you to sleep. Your doctor may also ask you to gargle with a local anesthetic or spray your throat with an anesthetic. Then, the doctor will insert the endoscope down your throat. Because of the sedative and the anesthetics, you should not feel any pain.

As the endoscope moves through your esophagus, you will be able to breathe normally. Although you will be awake, you will feel drowsy and will probably not be very aware of what is happening.

Your doctor will use the endoscope to examine your gastrointestinal tract. Your doctor may also decide to take a biopsy (tissue sample) so that he or she can look at tissue more closely under a microscope. If your doctor does do a biopsy, he or she will insert another instrument through your throat to remove the tissue. This should not be painful either.

When the test is done, you will still be sedated and will need someone to drive you home. After the sedative wears off, you may have a sore throat and experience some cramping. You will probably find that you don't remember very much about the procedure itself.

Sigmoidoscopy

Because it allows your doctor to view the rectum and lower colon, this test is especially effective in diagnosing and monitoring ulcerative colitis. Although it sounds uncomfortable, most people are surprised to find that it is less frightening than they imagined.

It is important that your bowel be empty for this procedure, so you will probably be on a clear liquid diet the night before the test. You may also need to do an enema about an hour before the test.

Doctors will occasionally give light sedatives to help people relax. But because there is usually not very much discomfort associated with the procedure, most doctors choose not to sedate their patients. Whether you receive sedation or not, you will be awake during the sigmoidoscopy.

For the test itself, you will lie on your side while the doctor inserts the sigmoidoscope into your rectum. Then, a little bit of air will flow through the scope into your bowel to widen the passage. This will probably be the most uncomfortable part of the procedure, making you feel bloated or cramped. You should not feel any pain as the sigmoidoscope moves into your intestine because the colon has very few nerve endings. After the test, which usually takes between five and fifteen minutes, you might feel cramped or bloated until the excess gas leaves your system.

Colonoscopy

A colonoscopy is the most complete endoscopic procedure. Using a long, flexible tube with a camera on the end, your doctor is able to view the entire large intestine and a portion of the small intestine. The test helps to identify inflamed areas, ulcers, abnormal growths, or bleeding.

Because you will be sedated for the procedure, the colonoscopy itself will not be as unpleasant as it might sound. Most people agree that the hardest part of a colonoscopy is the preparation. Before the test, you need to be on a clear liquid diet for at least a day to clean out your system. Sometimes, your doctor may ask you to consume only liquids for up to three days before the test.

In addition to being on a liquid diet, you will need to drink a bowel prep the day before the test. This helps to completely flush out your intestines and will cause you to have diarrhea. Some people have trouble sleeping the night before the test because they have to get up so often to use the bathroom.

For most people, however, the worst thing about the bowel prep is the taste of the drink. "The first colonoscopy I had, I wasn't that scared, because I was going to be asleep the whole time," says Monique. "But it was just that drink. I didn't think I was going to hold it down. So after I drank it, my mom gave me lemon and I squeezed it on my tongue. It kind of makes the awful taste go away, and it settles your stomach, too."

Before the colonoscopy, you will receive a sedative. Depending on your doctor's preferences, you may be entirely out for the procedure, or you may remain awake and very groggy. Your doctor will insert the scope through your rectum and guide it through your colon, examining intestinal tissue for problem areas. If necessary, he or she can take a biopsy as well.

If you are awake, you might feel some pressure and bloating as air enters your bowel through the scope, but you should not feel any pain. Afterward, you may have some cramping and bloating. But even if you were awake, you will probably find that you don't remember very much about the colonoscopy.

Computerized Tomography Scan

Computerized tomography (CT or CAT) scans give clear, detailed pictures of your digestive tract. If your doctor suspects that you have an abscess or another complication that doesn't show up well on X ray or with a scope, you may need to have a CT scan to tell for sure.

A CT scan is an X ray that uses a special, doughnut-shaped machine. The scan itself usually takes between five and fifteen minutes, but the preparation requires a little more time. You will probably need to drink a barium solution about an hour before having the scan so that your intestines will show up clearly in the X ray. In some cases, you may receive an injection of contrast solution instead of, or in addition to, the barium.

For the X ray, you will lie on a table that slides into the middle of the scanner. Because the scans are so sensitive, you have to lie very still and even hold your breath at times. The X rays are painless, but some people get claustrophobic from lying so still in a confined space. If small spaces bother you, be sure to mention this to your doctor (or the radiologist) ahead of time.

Magnetic Resonance Imaging (MRI)

MRI scans are generally used to detect and evaluate fistulas or abscesses in people with IBD. The scan uses a magnetic field, rather than X rays, to obtain detailed pictures of your internal organs. It is completely painless.

Before the test, you may have to drink a contrast solution to create clearer pictures of your digestive tract. You may also receive earplugs because the MRI scanner is loud. You will then lie on a table that slides into the tunnel-like scanner. The doctor and technologist performing the scan will probably leave the room, although they will be watching and communicating with you at all times from a separate room. You may be allowed to have a family member in the room with you, so if you are at all nervous about the test, ask about this possibility.

The MRI scanner will make a lot of hammering noises that are loud but completely normal. You will have to lie very still throughout the test and may need to hold your breath (for a few seconds) periodically. If you are claustrophobic, you should discuss this with your doctor before the test because you will be in a fairly small space for about 45 minutes. Your doctor can help you with relaxation techniques or will perhaps prescribe a mild sedative.

Ultrasound

Ultrasound, or sonography, is another method of diagnosing IBD and potential complications. Although most doctors do not consider it to be as accurate as endoscopy, ultrasound can help detect fistulas, strictures, and abscesses caused by Crohn's disease. It is a painless and relatively easy procedure.

Ultrasound uses sound waves, instead of X rays, to take pictures of your internal organs. Before the test, a doctor will rub a clear gel over your abdomen. Then he or she will guide an instrument called a transducer back and forth across the gelled area. The transducer sends out inaudible sound waves that bounce off your organs and back to the transducer. The ultrasound machine "translates" these sound waves into pictures that show up on a monitor. The whole thing usually takes just a few minutes.

Medical Treatments

Most people take a combination of drugs to treat Crohn's disease or ulcerative colitis. You may take one medication to help with diarrhea, one to fight bacteria in your intestines, and yet another for inflammation. It is not uncommon for people with IBD to take a handful of pills several times a day, even when they are not in the middle of a flare-up.

If you have a relatively mild case of IBD, however, your doctor may prescribe medications only during flare-ups. This is the case for Sue, who had surgery for Crohn's disease more than twenty years ago.

"I've had several episodes since the surgery, where I've had to go on prednisone for a while," she says. "But that usually takes care of it. And when I'm feeling OK, I don't take anything."

It may be tempting, if you're feeling well, to stop taking medications on your own. But this can be dangerous and pose serious risks to your health. It can also send you straight into a flare-up. Darcy made this mistake once and says she'll never do it again. "I tried not taking my meds once," she said. "I thought, 'I'm feeling fine. I'm stopping my meds.' And two months later, I started feeling bad again. My mom was like, 'Yeah, you were feeling fine because your medicines were working, honey.'"

Sometimes, finding the medication that works best for you takes time. For some reason, people respond very differently to the drugs that treat IBD. What works miracles for one person may do nothing to help another.

Talking with your doctor about what is helping and what isn't is a crucial part of managing your disease. Don't assume that just because your doctor has prescribed a certain medication, it is the only option. If a drug isn't effective for you, there may be a better choice.

Almost every medication carries risks and potential side effects. This chapter will discuss some of the more common side effects of common medications, but it is important that you talk to your doctor in more detail about any drugs you are taking. Monique and her parents recommend carefully reading the side effects before beginning any new medication. "We always sit down and read the side effects together," says Monique's mom. "That way, there aren't any surprises."

Anti-Inflammatory Drugs

These drugs help control the inflammation associated with IBD. Most anti-inflammatory drugs are used both to help put IBD into remission and to keep it in remission, which means that you will probably be on some type of anti-inflammatory medication even after your symptoms disappear.

There are three main types of anti-inflammatory drugs. Depending on the severity of your IBD and how well you respond to a particular medication, your doctor may want you to take just one of the following drugs or a combination to help keep your symptoms in check.

Sulfasalazine

Sulfasalazine (Azulfidine) is most effective in treating ulcerative colitis, but some patients with mild to moderate cases of Crohn's disease also respond well to the drug. It is made up of two parts: an aspirin-like component called 5-aminosalicylate (5-ASA) and another called sulfapyridine, which carries the 5-ASA to the inflamed areas of the bowel. The sulfapyridine causes most of the drug's side effects, which include nausea, sun sensitivity, and headache.

Sulfasalazine is best at controlling flare-ups when taken in large doses, which means you need to take pills several times a day. The same large dose is also necessary to keep IBD in remission once symptoms have gone away. Unfortunately, as the dosage increases, so do the side effects, and many people are ultimately unable to continue using the drug.

Dan was one of these people. When he was first diagnosed with Crohn's disease, he took sulfasalazine for several months before finally changing medications. "It made me extremely sensitive to the sun, and I got really bad headaches," he said. "It also made me look a little yellow."

Monique also experiences side effects from sulfasalazine, but she is able to tolerate them. "I got a doctor's note to take Tylenol at school whenever I need it," she says. "And that helps my headaches."

5-ASA Drugs

Asacol, Colazal, and Pentasa are basically the same as sulfasalazine, but without the sulfapyridine. Some doctors prefer prescribing 5-ASA drugs, especially for children and teenagers. These drugs work by time-releasing the 5-ASA into the inflamed portions of the intestine. Asacol and Colazal treat inflammation in the ileum and colon, and Pentasa treats inflammation in the small intestine and colon.

5-ASA drugs, which also come in suppository and enema forms, have fewer day-to-day side effects. They can, however, cause kidney problems in people who take large doses over a long period of time. This means that if you are taking one of these medications for long-term maintenance, it is a good idea to have annual exams to check the state of your kidneys.

Corticosteroids

Corticosteroids (prednisone, hydrocortisone, methylpred-nisolone) are used for more severe flare-ups and for patients who are not responding well to sulfasalazine or 5-ASA drugs. Corticosteroids can give quick results, relieve pain, and often bring IBD into remission. They also increase appetite, which can be a relief to someone who has not felt hungry in a long time. But corticosteroids are potent drugs that are not considered a long-term option for keeping IBD in remission.

Most people take corticosteroids in pill form. If you are hospitalized for a severe flare-up, however, you might receive large doses of corticosteroids intravenously, through an IV. The drugs are also available in suppository and enema forms, which may be prescribed for people with ulcerative colitis.

While the benefits of corticosteroids are undeniable, most people do not like the side effects, which include:

- Weight gain
- Puffiness and rounding of the face
- Acne
- Red marks or blotches on the skin
- Increased body and facial hair
- Mood swings

For some people, dealing with the side effects of corticosteroids is as challenging as dealing with the symptoms of IBD. "When I first started taking prednisone, I got a really bad moon face," says Sue. "I gained a lot of weight, which I didn't like. And it made me hungry. It was like someone flipped a switch from no appetite to huge appetite."

Although it is usually hard to avoid weight gain from corticosteroids, staying on a low-salt diet can help reduce some of the swelling. Monique, unhappy with the weight she was gaining on prednisone, found other ways to combat the problem. "I would want to snack because I'd get so hungry," she says. "And my doctor told me to drink lots of water, suck on Jolly Ranchers, or chew gum. And it did help. I wasn't quite so hungry then."

In addition to visible physical changes, corticosteroids carry other risks for those who use high doses over long periods of time. These include osteoporosis, diabetes, hypertension, cataracts, and growth problems. Because of this, most doctors recommend calcium supplements and periodic growth checks for children and young adults who use these drugs.

Usually, doctors will start to reduce your dosage when your symptoms have improved. But because these drugs affect your hormones, it is dangerous to stop taking them suddenly. You need to taper off slowly from the medication, taking smaller and smaller doses on a schedule prescribed by your physician.

Sometimes people become "steroid dependent," which means they are unable to go off of corticosteroids without having flare-ups. If this happens, your doctor may decide either to keep you on a small dose of the drug or to try an alternate medication.

In other cases, corticosteroids eventually fail to be effective in managing the disease. Dan took prednisone for several years, until it suddenly stopped working for him. "I was hospitalized during a flare-up, and they were pumping me full of as much prednisone as they could, but it wasn't working," he says. "We had to start talking about surgery or other options."

Immunomodulators

Drugs such as azathioprine (Imuran), 6-mercaptopurine (6-MP, Purinethol), and cyclosporine (Sandimmune,

Neoral) help suppress the immune system. Because the immune system appears to be at least partially responsible for causing the inflammation in IBD, immunosuppressants can help both in controlling flare-ups and in maintaining remission. They are most often prescribed for Crohn's disease, although some people take them for ulcerative colitis as well.

Doctors will usually prescribe azathioprine and 6-MP for patients who have not responded to treatment with anti-inflammatory drugs, or who have developed steroid-dependent disease. They are also used to treat perianal disease and fistulas.

While these drugs have fewer side effects than corticosteroids, they may cause allergic reactions (fever, rash, or achy joints), inflammation of the pancreas, and lowered white blood cell count. Another disadvantage is that they take from three to six months to start working, which usually means that you must be on other medications until they take effect.

Cyclosporine is another drug that may help people with severe cases of IBD who don't respond to standard treatments. Although clinical studies have shown it to be useful in treating both Crohn's disease and ulcerative colitis, it is not yet commonly used for IBD patients. This is partly because it is given intravenously, making it less convenient than other medications, and partly because it has potentially serious side effects, including kidney damage, high blood pressure, poor immunity to infection, and seizures. If you are taking cyclosporine, you will probably need regular checkups, every couple of weeks or so, to monitor your blood pressure and kidneys.

Antibiotics

Like immunomodulators, antibiotics help control immune response in the intestines. They also fight secondary infections that occur when bacteria gets into parts of the intestinal lining that have been damaged by IBD.

Metronidazole (Flagyl) can alleviate symptoms of flare-ups and also help heal fissures and fistulas. It is most effective in people with active cases of Crohn's disease affecting the colon. For some reason, it does not seem to be as useful for Crohn's of the small intestine or for ulcerative colitis. Side effects can include nausea, lack of appetite, headache, numbness in hands and feet, a metallic taste in your mouth, and vaginal yeast infections. Because of the way the drug interacts with alcohol, you should not consume alcoholic drinks while taking metronidazole.

If metronidazole doesn't work for you, your doctor may prescribe ciprofloxacin (Cipro) instead. Like metronidazole, it can help control flare-ups of Crohn's disease as well as treat fistulas.

Biologics

Biologic drugs are made from the products of living organisms. Although relatively new in the treatment of IBD, they are showing promise as an effective way to achieve and maintain remission in both Crohn's disease and ulcerative colitis.

Infliximab (Remicade), a biologic drug made from human and mouse DNA antibodies, received Food and Drug

Administration (FDA) approval as a treatment for Crohn's disease in 1998. It is the first medication specifically targeted for people with IBD. Infliximab blocks the production of a chemical called TNF-alpha, which may be partially responsible for causing the inflammation in IBD.

Doctors usually prescribe the medication for patients with moderate to severe cases of IBD who are not responding to other drugs. It can help improve symptoms or even put IBD into remission in a matter of weeks.

When Danny was eight years old and in the middle of a bad flare-up, he had the choice of having surgery or trying infliximab. "He was so young at the time," says his mom, Kathy. "Steroids weren't an option anymore, and we didn't want to do surgery if we didn't have to. So we tried infliximab, and he went into remission four days later."

Dan and Monique had similar experiences with the drug. Both chose to try infliximab instead of surgery, and both have had good results. Darcy, on the other hand, suffered an allergic reaction. "I did infliximab three times," she says. "The first time was awesome. The second time, I got flu-like symptoms. And the third time, I had a severe allergic reaction that put me in the hospital. It's a really rare reaction, but now I don't do infliximab anymore. It's too bad, because it really helped my stomach."

Infliximab is not available in pill form. It is given as an infusion (through an IV) that takes between two and three hours. Most patients receive three doses over a six-week span to start, and then get regular infusions every two months after that.

Because it is so new, there is not much information on the long-term side effects of infliximab. Most people seem to tolerate it very well. A minority experience allergic reactions like the one Darcy had, suffering from difficulty breathing, hives, or low blood pressure. Other people report problems with upper respiratory tract infections, cough, nausea, headache, or other infections after receiving infliximab.

Antidiarrheals

For a lot of IBD patients, running to the bathroom every thirty minutes or so is just a part of life. But antidiarrheal medications can help. Depending on your situation, your doctor may recommend using medications such as loperamide (Imodium) or diphenoxylate (Lomotil) to help relieve constant diarrhea.

Probably, even if you are using one of these medications, you will continue to experience some diarrhea. Although it might be tempting to use more than the recommended dosage of these drugs, you should stick to what your doctor has prescribed. Taking too much of an antidiarrheal can complicate IBD or result in dependency on the drug.

Pain Medications

Occasionally, during a flare-up, your doctor may prescribe some type of medication to help you manage the pain. Because most prescription pain medications are oral narcotics such as meperidine (Demerol) or oxycodone (Percocet, Percodan), they carry the risk of addiction and should not be used as a long-term solution.

Oral narcotics will not usually be as effective after a few weeks because you start building up a resistance. To achieve the desired effect, you have to start taking higher and higher doses. Eventually, your body becomes physically addicted, and you will experience withdrawal when you try to stop taking the drug. Trying to manage a drug addiction on top of IBD is not something most people want to think about.

That said, it is also important to remember that pain management can be part of having a chronic illness. It is possible and sometimes necessary to use medications in order to get through painful flare-ups. Responsible patients, following the guidance of their doctors, are able to use pain medication periodically without great risk.

Dan resisted medications to control his pain, afraid that he would become dependent on them. But finally, after being in and out of the hospital and waiting for new medications to take effect, he asked his doctor to prescribe something. "I avoided it for a long time," he says. "Now I've come to realize that it's sometimes necessary."

Surgery

According to the CCFA, approximately 60 to 75 percent of people with Crohn's disease and about 25 to 40 percent of people with ulcerative colitis need surgery at some point. While most people would prefer to avoid an operation if possible, the fact is that surgery can be a useful and often necessary means of treating IBD.

There are many reasons that people with IBD may need surgery, and several different types of surgery are common in the treatment of Crohn's disease and ulcerative colitis. Knowing as much as possible about the indications for surgery and the procedures themselves can make you feel more comfortable should you someday be faced with the decision.

Surgical removal of the colon is a cure for ulcerative colitis. By removing the colon (and sometimes the rectum), a surgeon is able to eliminate the source of the disease. If you have a bad case of ulcerative colitis that does not respond well to medication, your doctor may speak to you about the possibility of an operation.

Crohn's disease cannot be cured through surgery. Because it can affect any portion of the digestive tract, there is always a chance that Crohn's will reappear following an operation to remove part of the bowel. However, many people have found that surgery provides results that medicine cannot. In some cases, these results last a matter of months. In other cases, they last many years. Unfortunately, it is impossible to predict exactly how well surgery will work for you.

Reasons for Surgery

In many cases, surgery for IBD is elective. This means that it is up to you, your family, and your doctor to decide if surgery is the best option. Any of the following conditions may be reasons to discuss elective surgery:

⇒ Poor response to medicines

⇒ Appearance of cancer or pre-cancerous symptoms

⇒ Delayed growth

In addition, there are several situations in which surgery is required to control a complication related to IBD. These include:

⇒ Severe hemorrhaging

⇒ Bowel obstruction

⇒ Perforation (hole) in the bowel wall

⇒ Toxic megacolon (an extreme inflammation of the colon)

⇒ Development of abscesses or fistulas

The appearance of one of these complications does not necessarily mean that you will need emergency surgery. Hemorrhaging, small bowel obstruction, and fistulas only require surgery if they fail to respond to medicines; in most cases, surgery is not necessary. Perforation, toxic mega-colon, and abscesses, however, usually require some type of surgical treatment.

Making the Decision

Making the decision to proceed with surgery is not easy. If you are in the middle of a bad flare-up, it can be especially difficult, because you may be doing your best just to get through the days. For this reason, it is a good idea to think about surgery when you are symptom-free and able to research your options.

Because everyone is different, there are no simple answers as to when surgery is the best choice. In order to make the best possible decision, you might consider the following:

- Are there other options for treatment? Are there medications that might eliminate or postpone the need for surgery?

- Will it affect your quality of life? Is surgery likely to drastically improve the way you feel?

- Is there a chance of symptoms recurring? Is it likely that you will have flare-ups again? What are the chances of needing more surgery in the future?

- What are the risks involved? Do the benefits outweigh the risks?

⤳ What will be the changes in your day-to-day life? Will surgery mean that you have to change your lifestyle?

⤳ What are the types of surgery available? Do you have options?

If you are considering surgery, get as much information as possible. Read about different types of surgery, consult your doctor, get a second opinion, and, if possible, talk to people who have had the type of surgery in question. Your doctor may be able to give you the names of some people you can talk to, or you might call your local CCFA branch for referrals.

If you make the decision to have surgery, you will want to make sure you get the best surgeon for the job. Not all doctors have equal experience, and you should feel certain that you are in good hands. If you will be having a relatively new procedure, it is especially important to double-check that your surgeon knows what he or she is doing.

For more information on organizations that can help you with the decision about surgery and surgeons, see the Where to Go for Help section at the end of this book.

Resection

Resection is the most common operation for Crohn's disease. Your doctor might discuss the possibility of this procedure if your symptoms are not responding to other treatments, or if you develop a complication, such as bowel obstruction or an abscess.

During a resection, a surgeon makes an incision in your abdomen, removes the diseased section of your intestine, and reconnects the two ends of your bowel. If there are multiple problem areas, the surgeon may take out more than one segment of your intestine.

Resections are usually very effective for relieving symptoms. But there is always the chance that symptoms will show up again sometime in the future. According to the CCFA, 20 percent of people who have resections experience flare-ups again after two years. About 50 percent have symptoms five years after surgery. But of the people who have flare-ups again, only 40 to 50 percent need more surgery. Most, like Sue, are able to control their symptoms with medication.

Sometimes, however, people will need several repeat surgeries to remove more segments of their intestine. This can lead to a condition called short-bowel syndrome, which occurs when so much intestine has been removed that your body can no longer properly absorb nutrients. For more information on IBD and nutritional deficiencies, see chapter 5.

Strictureplasty

A stricture is a narrowed portion of intestine that can block the passage of intestinal contents and cause a great deal of pain. Strictures can be removed through resection, or they can be widened through a procedure called strictureplasty. Because strictureplasty does not involve removing any of the intestine, many doctors prefer to use this procedure, rather than resection, when possible.

To find the strictures, a surgeon will guide a small balloon, attached to a thin tube, through your intestine. When the balloon gets blocked, it means a stricture is present. The surgeon will widen the intestine at this point by cutting it open and reclosing it.

Whether or not you qualify for a strictureplasty will depend on a number of things, including the location and type of the strictures. If you have strictures that are particularly long, grouped closely together, or in your colon, strictureplasty may not be the best option.

Strictureplasty can be an effective way to battle bowel obstruction. There are no guarantees that new strictures won't develop, but in most cases, strictures do not reappear in locations where strictureplasty has already been performed.

Colectomy and Proctocolectomy

Colectomy is the removal of the colon. Proctocolectomy is the removal of the colon and the rectum. These operations are cures for ulcerative colitis. You may need one of these procedures if you have a severe case of ulcerative colitis that is not responding well to treatment, if you show signs of colon cancer, or if you develop serious complications such as perforation or toxic megacolon.

For people with Crohn's disease, colectomy or proctocolectomy might be an option if there is a lot of disease in the colon that is not responding to medication. However, since these procedures are not cures for Crohn's disease, most doctors will avoid them if possible.

When the colon and the rectum are removed, there must be an alternate path for fecal waste to leave the body. This can be achieved in several ways. Which method is best for you will depend on the nature of your IBD, your age, your health, your lifestyle, and your personal preferences.

Ileoanal Anastomosis (J-Pouch)

Also called the "pullthrough operation," ileoanal anastomosis is the most common surgical procedure for ulcerative colitis. In this operation, the colon and the rectum are removed, but the anal muscles stay in place. The surgeon then creates a new rectum, or pouch, from the ileum (the end of the small intestine), pulls down the pouch, and connects it to the anus.

Surgeons usually perform this operation in two parts. Because the new pouch needs time to heal before waste can pass through it, the surgeon generally creates a temporary "drainage system" called an ileostomy. This means that waste will leave your body through a hole in your abdomen. For the six to ten weeks that it takes the new pouch to heal, you will wear a disposable pouch to collect the waste that leaves your body through this hole, or stoma. When the healing is complete, the surgeon will close the ileostomy and reroute waste through the anus.

The main advantage to this type of surgery is that it eventually allows you to eliminate waste from your body normally. Your bowel movements may be more frequent than usual (five to eight a day) and will probably have a pasty appearance, but you will go to the bathroom in a more normal fashion.

The most common complication with ileoanal anastomosis is a condition called pouchitis, which is an inflammation of the new pouch. No one is really sure why pouchitis occurs, but it shows up in as many as 30 to 40 percent of people who undergo this type of surgery. It can cause diarrhea (sometimes bloody), abdominal pain, and fever. Usually, it clears up with antibiotics, although it sometimes reappears.

Standard Ileostomy

Before the ileoanal anastomosis was developed, this was the standard operation for ulcerative colitis. If your situation prevents you from having an ileoanal anastomosis, you may need an ileostomy instead. Some of the most common reasons for performing this operation rather than an ileoanal anastomosis are:

⮑ Rectal strictures or rectal cancer

⮑ Severe diarrhea

⮑ Malnourishment

In a standard ileostomy, the colon and usually the rectum and anal muscles are removed. Then the surgeon will close off the anal canal and reroute the ileum (the end of the small intestine) through a surgically created opening, or stoma. This means that waste will no longer pass through the anus, but through the stoma. Usually, the stoma is located on the right side of your abdomen, just below the belt line.

To collect the waste that exits your body, you will need to wear an ostomy pouch, which will attach to your skin with adhesive. There are several different types of pouches from which to choose, and your doctor and enterostomal therapy (ET) nurse will help you decide which will be easiest for you.

In some cases, a standard ileostomy can later be converted to an ileoanal anastomosis (if the rectum and anal muscles are left intact), or a continent ileostomy if your situation and health permit.

Continent Ileostomy

As an alternative to standard ileostomy, a continent ileostomy, or kock pouch, eliminates the need for an external pouch. Although this is an attractive possibility for many people who need an ileostomy, it is a complicated operation that is still fairly uncommon, especially as a first option.

In a continent ileostomy, the surgeon will remove the colon and rectum, and then create an internal pouch from the small intestine. This pouch allows waste to accumulate inside your body rather than outside. At regular intervals, you have to insert a small catheter (tube) through an opening in your abdomen to drain the contents of the pouch.

As with ileoanal anastomosis, the most common complication of this type of surgery is the development of pouchitis, which can cause abdominal pain, fever, and diarrhea.

Living with an Ostomy

For many people, the thought of having an ileostomy is frightening and even horrifying. Most people think that having an ostomy will mean drastic changes in their day-to-day life as well as in their relationships with other people. Some fear that they will never be able to live normally again.

Most people with IBD will never need an ileostomy at all. But if you do, you should not worry that it will make you any different. The truth is, once you learn the facts about having an ostomy, it will probably seem less upsetting than you thought.

First of all, keep in mind that you will probably feel better after an ileostomy than you've felt in a long time. If you have an ostomy to cure ulcerative colitis, you will end your battle with IBD! Most people who have ostomy surgery find that they have more energy and are able to do more things than they could do before the operation.

If you have an ostomy, you should still be able to do all of the following things:

↩ Participate in most sports, including swimming

↩ Eat the same foods you ate before surgery

↩ Engage in sexual activities

↩ Have children

↩ Wear the same types of clothes that you wore before surgery

↩ Bathe and shower normally

People who have ostomy surgery should refrain from heavy lifting and contact sports. Depending on your particular situation, your doctor may suggest other restrictions as well. However, you are usually able to do pretty much everything that you could before surgery.

A common concern that many people have about ostomy pouches is that they will leak or smell bad. This is not the case. Ostomy pouches are generally odor-free. If you do experience problems, there are several things that you can use to eliminate odor, including pouch deodorizers and oral medications. As far as leaking, as long as you empty your pouch regularly, you should not encounter this problem.

Of course, you will need to learn how to take care of your ostomy pouch and the skin that surrounds the stoma. But with the assistance of your doctor and your ET nurse, you will probably find that, after the initial adjustment, life with an ostomy is not difficult.

If you are having problems with the pouch system you are using, talk to your doctor or ET nurse right away. There are many types of pouch systems available, and there is no reason that you should use one that isn't working for you.

Laparoscopic Surgery

Laparoscopic, or keyhole, surgery is one of the newest developments in the surgical treatment of IBD. At this time, it is only used for certain types of operations, most commonly resection and colectomy with standard ileostomy.

In a laparoscopic operation, the surgeon inserts a tiny video camera through a small incision in your abdomen. The camera gives the surgeon a magnified view of your abdominal cavity, enabling him or her to see things in great detail and eliminating the need to create a large incision. Using specialized surgical instruments inserted through another tiny incision, the surgeon is able to perform the needed procedure.

Because the incisions in laparoscopic surgery are so much smaller than in traditional surgery, recovery time is generally much shorter. People who have laparoscopic surgery are usually able to leave the hospital earlier and return to normal diet and activities sooner than those who have traditional surgery. But laparoscopic surgery is also more expensive, requires more surgical expertise, and takes longer to perform than traditional surgery. If you are considering laparoscopic surgery and want more information, see the Where to Go for Help section at the end of this book.

Before and After Surgery

Preparation for surgery will vary from case to case, depending on the severity of your illness, your overall health, and the type of surgery you have. If you are having emergency surgery, you will probably not have much time to prepare for the operation. On the other hand, if your surgery is elective, you can expect some standard procedures, which can take anywhere from a day or two to several weeks.

Because surgery is most successful if you are properly nourished, you may need to follow a special diet before the operation. If you are having trouble eating solid foods, you might drink a liquid diet or elemental diet (see chapter 5) for a few days.

You may also need to discontinue use of certain types of medications, such as immunomodulators, before surgery.

If you are taking corticosteroids, you will continue to receive this medication intravenously before and after the surgery. Your doctor might also give you antibiotics to help counter any infections.

Finally, most surgical procedures for IBD require that your bowels be empty. This will mean taking an enema and possibly drinking a bowel prep solution similar to those used for endoscopies.

Your recovery time will depend on the type of surgery. You can most likely expect to be in the hospital for about a week and out of school or work for at least another three weeks. You may have some pain in the area of the incision and, if you have for Crohn's disease, some diarrhea. The most common complication with any type of surgery is infection, so if you experience a fever at any time, you should notify your doctor.

Diet and Nutrition

Although you cannot cure IBD by eating, or not eating, certain foods, you may find that your eating habits affect the way you feel. Some people with IBD are so sensitive to particular types of food that they avoid them altogether. Others don't have problems with food at all and eat whatever they like.

Whether you follow a special diet or not, you should be aware of the ways in which IBD can affect your nutritional health. Getting the right nutrients will ensure that you grow as you should and that your medications are able to work properly. It will also contribute to your overall health, which can make you feel better all around.

If you are considering a significant diet change, you should first consult your doctor or a registered nutritionist. Your specific dietary needs will depend on your age, your weight, your lifestyle, and the type of IBD that you have. An expert will be able to evaluate your nutritional needs and recommend the type of diet that will work best for you.

IBD and Nutrition

The most obvious way that IBD can affect nutrition is that it decreases your appetite. Most people with active cases of Crohn's disease or colitis do not feel like eating very much. "When I have bad flare-ups, I have no appetite," says Dan. "I can go for a couple of days without eating anything and not even realize it."

Although appetite usually improves as medication brings symptoms under control, eating too little can lead to extreme weight loss and to growth problems in children and teens. Because stunted growth is also a side effect of some medications used to treat IBD, this can become a serious problem.

Even when you have a good appetite, IBD may impair your ability to absorb essential nutrients. Your body takes in nutrients through the small intestine, so inflammation in this area, which is common in Crohn's disease, makes it more difficult for your body to absorb them. People who have had parts of their small intestine surgically removed can have special difficulties getting necessary nutrients and may need nutritional supplements.

Other nutritional risks with IBD include iron deficiency, common in ulcerative colitis and Crohn's colitis; mineral deficiencies and dehydration from chronic diarrhea; and vitamin B-12 deficiency, especially when the ileum is affected. In addition, some medications used to treat IBD can interfere with the digestive process, making it even more difficult to get the nutrients you need.

This does not mean, however, that you are necessarily at risk for malnutrition. Most people with IBD, especially those with moderate cases and those who have never undergone surgery, do not ever develop nutritional problems. The people who do can usually get all the necessary nutrients by eating well and taking supplements.

Tips for Healthy Eating

Although everyone should eat well, it is especially important for people with IBD. But eating healthfully does not have to mean following a special, restrictive diet. It can be as simple as following some general guidelines.

Eat a Variety of Good Food

The U.S. Department of Agriculture's (USDA's) dietary recommendations, which you may know as the food pyramid, are designed for an average, healthy person. If you do not have difficulties eating a particular type of food and if your doctor agrees, this general diet has several benefits. It encourages you to eat healthy foods from a variety of sources, increasing the chances that you will receive the nutrients you need. It also helps limit your intake of greasy, fatty, and sugary foods, which can aggravate IBD.

Listed below are the recommended dietary allowances (RDAs):

Grains: 6–11 servings a day
(One serving = 1 slice of bread, 1 ounce cereal, or 1 cup rice or pasta)

Fruits: 2–4 servings a day
(One serving = 1 piece of fruit, 1 cup juice, or 1 cup canned fruit)

Vegetables: 3–5 servings a day
(One serving = 1 cup raw or cooked vegetables or 1 cup leafy raw vegetables)

Dairy: 2–4 servings a day
(One serving = 1 cup milk or yogurt, 1 to 2 ounces cheese)

Meats: 2 servings a day
(One serving = 1 to 3 ounces lean meat, poultry, or fish, 2 eggs, or 1 cup cooked beans)

Fats and Oils: Use sparingly
(Includes sugary, high-fat, and fried foods)

Eat Small Meals

Eating enough food to meet the RDAs may seem impossible, especially to someone with IBD. During flare-ups, most people do not feel hungry enough to eat even half of the recommended servings. When you are not sick, however, remember that a serving is usually less than you think. By eating a ham and cheese sandwich with a slice of tomato, you can get two servings of grains, one of meat, one of dairy, and one of vegetables.

It may also be helpful to eat only small portions at a time. Instead of three large meals, try eating several small meals throughout the day. Healthy snacking can be a good way to get enough food without overloading your bowels with too much at once.

Drink Water

Chronic diarrhea increases your risk of dehydration because it quickly depletes your body's supply of water.

Dehydration makes you weak and tired, and can put you at risk for kidney stones. Most experts recommend drinking 64 ounces (about 8 cups) of water per day, and your doctor may want you to drink even more to compensate for extra water you lose.

Enjoy Your Food

Many people with IBD come to think of food as their enemy. The more you end up doubled over in pain after meals, the more tempting it may be to avoid eating altogether. But if you're too stressed about eating, it can actually make digestion more difficult. Finding foods that you can easily tolerate and enjoy is important in managing IBD.

Common Aggravators

Although everyone is different, there are some foods that commonly cause problems for people with IBD. You may find that eliminating some or all of these foods from your diet will make you more comfortable, especially during flare-ups. On the other hand, unless you are sure of difficulties with things such as fruits and vegetables or whole grains, you should not rush to cut them out of your diet, as they provide a lot of nutritional benefit.

Some of the things that can aggravate the symptoms of IBD are:

⇨ Caffeine (this includes chocolate!)

⇨ Raw fruits and vegetables

➯ Seeds, nuts, and popcorn

➯ Sugary foods

➯ Fried or fatty foods

➯ Whole grains

➯ Beer

The best bet for discovering exactly what you can and cannot tolerate is to work with your doctor or a registered nutritionist. They can assist you with methods of precisely identifying the foods that cause problems for you.

Special Diets for IBD

At some point, you may need to follow a special diet. Some IBD diets are short-term, either to prepare for a test procedure or to alleviate pain during a bad flare-up. Others are long-term attempts to eliminate problematic foods from your diet.

Like so many aspects of IBD, no one diet is right for everyone. Through experimentation, you may discover that the best solution for you is to combine several diets or create one of your own. This was the case for Dan, who tried a few diets without success. Finally, he decided to combine several different diets into one. "Whenever I cut out one type of food or another, it didn't seem to help at all," he says. "But then I cut out all of those things together, and it really made a difference."

If you do decide to follow a certain diet, make sure that you communicate with your doctor first. And don't be discouraged if the first thing you try doesn't work. Sometimes it takes several tries to discover the specific combination of foods that you can and cannot tolerate.

The following are descriptions of some general diets commonly used for IBD. For a list of books dealing in-depth with the subject of diet and nutrition for IBD, see the For Further Reading section at the end of this book.

Liquid Diets

Liquid diets are usually short-term. If you are scheduled to have an endoscopic procedure, are recovering from surgery, or are having a particularly bad flare-up, you may need to eat only liquids for a while. Liquid diets help to clear out your system and to give your bowels a rest. A clear liquid diet consists of clear broth, decaffeinated beverages, fruit juices, and gelatin. A full liquid diet includes the same things as a clear liquid diet, plus milk, eggs, puddings, ice cream, vegetable juices, and sometimes even strained meats.

If you are on a liquid diet for any length of time or if your doctor is concerned about your weight or other nutritional issues, you may also drink a commercial formula that is specially designed to provide you with all of the nutrients you need.

Low-Fiber Diets

Many people with IBD have a hard time digesting high-fiber foods. When the intestine becomes inflamed and narrows, these foods can cause considerable irritation and pain. As a result, some people find it helpful to eliminate foods such as raw fruits and vegetables, nuts, seeds, popcorn, whole grains, and beans from their diets, at least temporarily. If you are on a low-fiber diet, you may be able to return to your regular eating habits when your flare-up ends.

Low-Fat Diets

Like fiber, fat is often hard to digest. If you have Crohn's disease in your small intestine, you may have extra difficulties absorbing fats. Eating fatty foods will leave you feeling uncomfortable. If you are on a low-fat diet, you will need to avoid fried and sugary foods and should stick to lean meats and low-fat dairy products. As with a low-fiber diet, you should follow your doctor's recommendations for continuing the diet when your IBD is not active.

High-Calorie Diets

If you have lost a lot of weight or are not growing as you should, your doctor may prescribe a high-calorie diet. This will usually include meats, whole dairy products, and enriched grains as well as plenty of fruits and vegetables. High-calorie diets may be modified after you've successfully gained and maintained a healthy weight, or your doctor may wish to keep you on the diet long-term.

Lactose-Free Diets

Some people with IBD are also lactose-intolerant, which means that they have difficulties digesting dairy products. If you notice bloating and cramping after eating dairy products, your doctor may recommend a lactose-tolerance test to see if this is true for you.

Being lactose-intolerant does not necessarily mean that you will have to give up all dairy products, although this is one option. Another, often preferable, alternative is to take lactase supplements along with dairy foods, to help with their digestion. This allows you to continue getting nutritional benefits from dairy without the painful side effects. Your doctor or nutritionist should guide you in deciding how best to handle your diet.

Nutritional Supplements

Even if there isn't any evidence that you have nutritional deficiencies, your doctor may suggest taking a daily multivitamin as a precaution, especially during flare-ups. Some people with severe cases of IBD, or people who have undergone surgery, need to take additional supplements as well.

If you are at risk for vitamin B, vitamin D, or calcium deficiency as a result of acute IBD, medications, or surgery, you will probably need to take supplements to make up for what your body cannot naturally absorb. Iron deficiency, which is common in ulcerative colitis and Crohn's disease affecting the colon, can be corrected through supplements as well.

TEN and TPN

These two forms of nutritional therapy, also called "elemental diets" or "tube feeding," involve delivering nutrients directly into your stomach or bloodstream. This is usually a short-term solution reserved for the following situations:

- Severe cases of IBD that do not respond to medication

- Extreme weight loss or growth problems

- Preparation for or recovery from surgery

- Poor absorption of nutrients because large sections of intestine have been surgically removed

If you go on nutritional therapy, you will receive all of your nutrition from a specially formulated and easily digestible liquid diet. Because of the taste of these formulas, you cannot drink them as you might an ordinary liquid diet. The food must be delivered directly into your system.

In most cases, this is achieved through what is called total enteral nutrition (TEN). This means that the nutrients are going directly into your stomach or small intestine, through a tube that is inserted through your nose or directly into an opening in your abdomen. Usually, feedings take place at night and the tube comes out during the day, but sometimes it is necessary to keep the tube in place throughout the day as well.

Being fed through a tube can be an alarming idea, and it usually takes people at least a few days to get used to the process. Unless you are hospitalized while you are getting TEN, you or a family member will have to learn to insert and remove the tube, and this can be frightening as well.

The good news about nutritional therapy is that it can work wonders. People with severe flare-ups, who would otherwise have no option except surgery, often go into remission after a few weeks of TEN. And children and teens experiencing stunted growth or delayed sexual development can see improvement after just short-term nutritional therapy as well.

An alternative to TEN is a process called total parenteral nutrition (TPN), which bypasses your digestive system altogether and delivers nutrients straight into your bloodstream. A catheter is inserted into a vein in your chest, and food travels directly through the catheter. Because this process is more complicated than TEN, it is usually administered in a hospital. However, people with severe cases of IBD or severe nutritional problems may require ongoing TPN therapy and must learn to perform the process at home.

Living with a Restricted Diet

Whether you are just a little more careful about what you eat, following a diet prescribed by your doctor, or getting nutritional therapy, adjusting to a new diet can be frustrating. Giving up your favorite foods or trying to find something you can eat when you go to a restaurant isn't easy. But most people find that, after a while, it becomes easier.

Monique is bothered by lactose and has had to give up dairy products. "The milk was the hardest thing," she says. "I used to drink two gallons just by myself. Now I drink milk that's lactose-free. And when we order pizza, we get one without cheese for me. It just has sauce and toppings. It's really good, actually. I like it better that way."

For Dan, the hardest part of changing his diet was eating in restaurants. "At first, I used to get really mad," he says. "I'd look at the menu and see this long list of stuff I couldn't eat. But now I'm used to it, and since I know that not eating those foods makes me feel better, it's worth it."

Emotional Aspects

Everyone reacts differently to IBD. Some people view it merely as an inconvenience that occasionally disrupts their lives. For others, it is a source of great frustration, embarrassment, and possibly even serious depression.

The emotional aspects of a chronic disease can be just as difficult to live with as the physical ones. This is especially true because the fatigue, pain, and other stresses of IBD can make you less willing to sort out all of your feelings, much less deal with them. "Sometimes," says Dan, "you just want to forget you have this problem. Or at least not think about it."

Although it may be tempting to live in denial, finding ways to deal with anger, embarrassment, or feelings of loneliness and isolation is as important as taking the proper medications. There is evidence to suggest that emotional stress can aggravate IBD, so ignoring these problems may actually make you sicker.

There are many ways to cope emotionally with the stress of Crohn's disease and ulcerative colitis. This chapter includes suggestions from people who have firsthand experience dealing with the emotional challenges of IBD.

Embarrassment

"I didn't tell my friends about the colitis for a while," says Monique, "but my good friends know now. I tell my friends so they kind of know what's going on, but I don't really get into details . . . because who wants to talk about all the details?"

Because of the nature of IBD, many people are uncomfortable discussing it with others. If this is true for you, and you don't want to get into all the details of IBD, you will probably find that a simple explanation is enough to satisfy most people.

Dan didn't tell his coworkers that he had Crohn's disease until they started commenting on all the weight he had lost. "It was a little uncomfortable at first," he says, "but usually I just told them that I had an intestinal disease, and that was good enough. A few people asked for more details, but most didn't."

With the exception of your family members and your doctor, most people don't need to know anything more about IBD than what you are comfortable telling them. At first, you may not want to say much more than, "I have Crohn's disease (or ulcerative colitis). It's an intestinal illness that causes a lot of pain."

As you become more used to living with IBD, it may become easier to talk about. Still, it's up to you which details you want to discuss with which people. You should not feel that you have to explain more than you want to just because someone asks. "Know that you don't have to be an open book about it," says Jessica.

Many people, however, find that being open about IBD is an important part of managing it. "I'm really an advocate of talking about things," says Darcy. "I don't even want to think about where I'd be if I hadn't ended up talking to someone. I really recommend finding that person that you can open up to, because it makes such a difference."

Another common source of embarrassment is diarrhea. If you are like most people with Crohn's or colitis, you probably spend a lot of time running to the bathroom. This can be embarrassing, especially if you are worried that everyone is watching you.

If you are in school, communicate with your teachers. Let them know that you may have to leave class frequently to use the bathroom, and arrange to do this as quietly as possible. "In elementary and middle school, when I was more bothered by all this, my mom or I went to the teacher at the beginning of the year to say, 'Here's what's going on,'" says Dustin. "We explained that if I had to go to the bathroom, I had to go. You don't want to stop class all the time, so you just sit down with the teacher and explain things."

Sometimes, the treatments for IBD can make you feel conspicuous as well. If you have surgery, are on nutritional therapy, or are experiencing visible side effects from medications, people may ask a lot of questions. "I still have a nasty scar on my chest from a TPN catheter," says Dustin. "So I still have to explain it now."

Keep in mind that, in most cases, people are either just curious or are concerned about you, or both. Still, it is up to you how much to tell them. Start with what makes you comfortable, and work up to more when you feel ready. Usually, you will find that people are supportive and want to help.

Anger and Frustration

"I remember when I was first diagnosed I would get really frustrated thinking about all the tests and medications that I had to take when I was still so young," says Dan. "And when I'm really sick, I still get frustrated sometimes, because I don't like people having to help me all the time. I feel like I should be able to take care of myself now. But sometimes I just need a little help, and I've had to get used to that."

Knowing that you will always have IBD can be frustrating. It can also be frustrating to run to the bathroom all day long, or miss school or work, or feel so tired that you have to stay in bed rather than do something you enjoy. Nevertheless, most people find that these things become easier to accept over time. "So much depends on attitude," says Sue. "You'll have your bad days, but good days, too. It's not the end of the world. It's just something you have to learn to live with."

Other things associated with IBD can affect your moods as well. Monique experienced mood swings when she took certain medications. "I'd read about the side effects, so I knew why I was getting so mad," she says. "But sometimes I'd just have to put on my head-phones and listen to music or go to my room and read until I felt better. If I was with my friends, I'd just tell them that I had to sit there a minute and calm myself down."

Although it is sometimes hard to think about anything but the fact that you are sick, you will probably find that you are happiest when you are able to concentrate on something else. "Find something you enjoy doing and devote your time to it," says Dustin. "The more you devote your time to something else, the better it's going to be."

Depression

"After I was diagnosed with Crohn's, I got very depressed," says Darcy. "I was in pain. I hated the way I looked. Even just the word 'disease' freaked me out. The first year, I basically let Crohn's take over my life. I was a shut-in in my own house."

Although it is normal to sometimes feel angry, frustrated, and sad when you have a disease like IBD, some people develop clinical depression, which is a serious condition. You should seek professional counseling if you experience any of the following:

- Suicidal thoughts

- Complete loss of interest in your friends and other activities for more than two weeks

- A depressed mood that is especially intense and lasts for two weeks or longer without improvement

- Dramatic and worrisome changes in your thoughts, feelings, or behaviors

Even if you don't suspect clinical depression, you may benefit from speaking with a professional. If you are interested in talking to someone who can help, ask your parents to help you find a counselor. Some ways that you can find professional help are to:

- ➭ Ask your doctor to recommend a mental health counselor.

- ➭ Talk to a school counselor or ask him or her for a referral.

- ➭ Call city mental health hotlines that are listed in the phone book.

- ➭ Call the psychology departments of local universities.

- ➭ Ask friends or family to recommend a good counselor.

Like any doctor, a counselor should be someone with whom you feel comfortable. "Not everybody that you talk to will be a good match," says Dr. Fiona Vajk. "Trust your instincts, and don't be afraid to switch counselors."

You might also consider contacting the nearest branch of the Crohn's and Colitis Foundation of America (CCFA). Most local branches offer support groups so that you can discuss IBD with others who are going through the same things. For more information on the CCFA, see the Where to Go for Help section at the back of this book.

Feeling Misunderstood

Because IBD is a so-called invisible disease, it is sometimes hard for other people to understand. Unless you suddenly lose or gain a lot of weight, or show other outward signs of illness, people may even have a hard time accepting the fact that you are sick.

"Before I got diagnosed with Crohn's, I think my siblings thought I was a whiner," says Darcy. "They thought I just wanted attention. And my teachers had trouble believing I was really sick. I'm not the kind of person who likes to show when I'm in pain, so I'd miss a lot of school and then come back and put on a happy face. And the teachers would say things like, 'Oh, you finally came back to class.'"

Sometimes, even doctors can be skeptical that there is anything really wrong with you, and it may take a long time to convince them otherwise. "It took them more than a year to find out that I had Crohn's," says Dan. "I was told that I had everything from stress to food poisoning, but no one believed it was anything more serious until they finally did a colonoscopy. It was really frustrating, knowing that there was something wrong, but being told that there wasn't."

It is normal for people with any chronic illness to feel that no one really understands what they are going through. And the truth is, even after you have a name for your troubles, most people don't understand what it means to have IBD. But that doesn't mean that they are uninterested or incapable of support, if you give them a chance. Try talking openly to someone you trust, whether it is a friend, a family member, or a teacher, and you might find that he or she surprises you by understanding more than you thought.

If you have tried talking to people about IBD and still feel like they don't grasp it, you may want to seek out people who will definitely understand what you are feeling. Contact the CCFA to find out about local support groups for people with IBD, go online to find IBD chat rooms and discussion boards, or ask your doctor about other resources for people with IBD or other chronic illnesses.

When Danny won a CCFA Local Hero Award, and met other kids with IBD for the first time, it gave him a sense of community. "He got a lot more confidence after that," says his mom. "For the first time, he got the bigger picture, that there were lots of people out there who had it."

Many teens have found support and made lasting friendships through camps offered by CCFA. Darcy was reluctant to attend a camp for kids with IBD, but says that the people she met there changed her life. "I thought it would be a bunch of people whining about how much their stomachs hurt," she says. "My parents basically dragged me there. But it was amazing. Everyone knew exactly what I was going through, and when it was over, I seriously did not want to leave."

Body Image

"Crohn's has made me not grow as much," says Jessica. "I've always been smaller than my friends."

If you have had growth problems related to IBD or if you've taken corticosteroids such as prednisone that have caused you to gain a lot of weight, you may have felt awkward about your body at some point or another. Whether you feel that you are too small or too big, this is not an easy thing to handle.

"When I first got Crohn's, my weight tended to fluctuate by at least 60 or 70 pounds when I flared up," says Dan. "First I'd lose a lot of weight and then I'd puff up from the prednisone. People notice that type of thing. And frankly, it's even hard to dress when your weight is going all over the place."

Another thing that can cause people with IBD to be unhappy with their bodies is the unpleasant nature of the disease itself. When you are constantly thinking about your bowels, as well as being exhausted and in pain, it can be difficult to see yourself as attractive.

It may take some time, but most people eventually learn to accept the physical changes that come with IBD. Remember that people see the image that you project. When you are comfortable with the way you look, people respond to that confidence. Other people with IBD offer some additional tips for improving your body image:

- Think about how much your body has been through, and what it is able to endure. The fact that you deal with a chronic illness means that you are strong.

- When you feel up to it, stay physically active.

- Remember that most weight loss or gain from IBD is temporary and beyond your control.

- Recognize that other people are not as concerned about the way you look as you are.

- Find other people who have gone through the same thing and talk to them for support.

If you find yourself regularly rejecting food because you are afraid it will make you gain more weight, are obsessing about food, or are avoiding contact with others because of the way you feel about your appearance, you might benefit from professional counseling. It's normal to experience some anxiety over body image, even when you don't have a chronic illness, but this anxiety should not reach the point where it starts to take over your life.

Stress

Finding ways to deal successfully with stress in your life can be powerful tools in managing IBD. Many people find that stressful incidents can trigger flare-ups or make existing flare-ups worse. Dustin has noticed that his flare-ups usually occur at the end of the school year, around finals time. "People keep telling me it's stress-related," he says, "and I can see that. But I don't know for sure."

Whether or not you feel your flare-ups are connected to stress, you will almost certainly experience more stress during the times that your disease is active. The physical pain, emotional response to getting sick, and interference in your daily life are enough to make anyone feel stressed out. But there are some things you can do to take control:

- Identify the source of stress. Is it a specific problem you can solve?

- Communicate your feelings to family and friends. Opening up to other people can help relieve pent-up stress.

- Ask others for help when you need it. Don't try to do too much, especially when you are in the middle of a flare-up.

- Make time for activities you enjoy. Taking time for yourself is crucial.

- When possible, engage in physical activity. Exercise of any type is a stress-reliever.

↬ Try yoga, deep breathing, or other relaxation techniques.

↬ Find something to laugh about. Watching a funny movie or talking with a friend who always makes you laugh will help relieve tension.

There is no such thing as a stress-free life. But it's important to manage stress as much as possible, keeping it at a tolerable level. Knowing ahead of time which stress-management techniques work for you can help you deal with increased levels of stress when your disease flares up.

Uncertainty About the Future

If you are worried about how IBD will affect the rest of your life, you are not alone. Most people spend a lot of time thinking about the future. Having a chronic disease adds another big question mark into the equation.

The good news is that IBD should not prevent you from completing school, getting a job, marrying, having kids, traveling, playing sports, or doing any of the other things that you may want to do. You might have to work a little harder to achieve some of these things than if you did not have IBD. Or you might find that IBD has little impact on your daily life at all.

Dan, who has had Crohn's disease for more than ten years, says that it has not prevented him from doing the things he considers most important. "Sometimes I can't be as physically active as I want," he says. "But that's just something I've had to get used to."

As with most things, attitude plays a big part in how much you are able to accomplish with IBD. Darcy feels that her change in attitude toward Crohn's disease has made all the difference. "My doctors call me the Crohn's Poster Child now, because I'm so positive," she says. "I still have times when I'm like, 'Oh, poor me. I'm going to have this disease the rest of my life.' Because there's just no way of knowing what the future's going to be like. But you have to live your life."

Tips for Daily Life

Most people, when they are first diagnosed with IBD, want to know exactly how the disease will affect their daily lives. Unfortunately, since Crohn's disease and ulcerative colitis affect everyone a little differently, this is impossible to predict. This chapter will discuss some of the more common challenges and concerns, as well as suggestions for how to manage them.

Anticipating how you will deal with the following situations can make you feel more confident, more prepared, and more in control of your life. You may find that you have to think about things that you once took for granted or even make some changes in your daily routine. But in most cases, as with most aspects of IBD, adjustment is the hardest part. Once you get used to life with Crohn's or colitis, you will probably find that you are able to manage better than you might have thought.

Bathroom Trips

One of the biggest worries among people with IBD is the need to use the bathroom at an inopportune time. If you are in a restaurant, store, or other public place, it is a good idea to find out where the bathroom is as soon as you get there. Get to know the locations of bathrooms in local malls and shopping centers, and ask to use an "employee-only" rest room if you really need it. Most often, if you tell someone, "I have to use a bathroom now," they'll let you without asking any questions.

If you're in school, arranging a system for bathroom use can be helpful. Ask your teachers for permission to go to the rest room whenever you need to, without having to call attention to yourself each time. Monique did this, and it worked well for her.

"It was less embarrassing than having to ask to go to the bathroom all the time," she says. "If any of the other kids asked me why I could go whenever I wanted, I just said, 'Because I can.'"

Although it may be tempting sometimes, you shouldn't let a fear of accidents stop you from going out in public. "During a bad flare-up, if you're really worried, keep an extra pair of underwear and pants with you," says Dan. "You probably won't ever have to use them, but it'll make you feel better."

If your doctor agrees, you might also try using an antidiarrheal medicine, especially when you know it will be more difficult to find a bathroom. "I have a lot of diarrhea," says Sue. "But it's nothing that's been debilitating for me or kept me from doing anything. Imodium will help me, so if I know I'm going to go out to play golf or something, I'll take that."

Managing Pain

Unfortunately, short of taking medication, there is sometimes little you can do about the pain that comes with a bad flare-up. But there are ways that you can ease your discomfort.

A lot of people find that the most powerful weapon against pain is to concentrate on other things. "For me, the biggest thing is not to sit around and think about it," says Darcy. "And it's hard, sometimes, because you don't exactly feel like getting up and doing anything. But I watch a movie or play around on the computer or read a book. Anything that keeps me from thinking about the pain and just feeling sorry for myself."

Other suggestions that people with IBD offer for dealing with pain are:

➼ Hot baths

➼ Sitting still in an upright position

➼ Keeping your feet up

➼ Sleeping with a pillow on your stomach

If nothing else helps, try to remember that the pain will eventually end. Concentrating on the fact that your symptoms will improve can help get you through the worst times. "You're not going to feel this way forever," Darcy says. "It does get better."

Adjusting at School

Keeping up with classes can be challenging when you're in the middle of a flare-up. Like any illness, IBD may cause you to miss some days at school. It may also make your days in school more difficult, especially if you are always rushing off to the bathroom or in pain. By making some simple adjustments, though, most students with IBD are able to manage school.

Communicating with counselors and teachers is crucial. Although you may be reluctant to call attention to yourself or your situation, it is important to let school officials know why you are frequently absent or having difficulties keeping up with your work.

Monique, who missed a lot of school during a bad flare-up, was concerned about how this would affect her grades. In order to help, her mom wrote a personalized letter to each of her teachers, explaining the situation. She also sent the teachers several brochures from the CCFA, which explained IBD in more detail. "It made a real difference," says her mom, Angie.

Depending on your situation and how much IBD inter-feres with your schooling, you may find it helpful to fill out a 504 form. It explains your condition as a disability and qualifies you for necessary accommodations. It is available through the main office of your school or school district.

The first year that she was sick, Monique and her par-ents chose not to fill out a 504. The next year, they changed their minds. "At first, I didn't want to fill out any special paperwork," says her mom. "I was afraid it would go on her record. But it was a nightmare. The teachers didn't send home her homework, and no one knew what was going on with her. The next year we filled out the form, and it's been great."

In addition to ensuring she got any missed assignments on time, the 504 enabled Monique to make a few adjust-ments to her normal school routine. "The counselor arranged my classes so they were all close together, and

I got to pick out a locker near my classes and the bathroom," she says. She also requested a second set of books to keep at home, so that she could keep up with assignments when she missed school.

Whether or not you choose to apply for a 504, be sure to communicate your needs to someone at school who is in a position to help you. This might be a teacher, a counselor, the principal, or the school nurse. Most people find that with persistence, they are able to work out arrangements that make it easier to keep up with class work.

Dining Out

If you have to watch what you eat or are on a special diet, eating out can be a frustrating and even anxiety-provoking experience. Whether you are dining at someone else's house, at school, or at a restaurant, a little advanced planning can make a big difference in how much you are able to enjoy your meal.

Eating at a Friend's Home

Following a strict diet or being on a liquid diet makes accepting dining invitations tricky, especially if your host doesn't know about your dietary restrictions. How do you politely tell someone what you are and aren't able to eat? Or should you not mention it and hope for the best?

Every situation is different. If you know the person well enough, it's probably easiest to be upfront about what you can and cannot eat. Your host will appreciate the fact that you felt comfortable enough to be honest and may even be relieved that he or she didn't prepare something you couldn't enjoy.

If you feel uncomfortable asking for special accommodations (or wouldn't be able to eat anything at all, since you are on a liquid diet or TEN), you have several options:

- Accept the invitation and assume there will be something you can eat.

- Accept the invitation and say, "But I'm on a restrictive diet for health reasons and don't want to trouble you, so I'll bring along something I can eat, if that's OK." (You may find that your host will then offer to prepare something special anyway.)

- Politely decline the invitation and invite the person to your house instead.

As easy as it might be to regularly decline invitations because you are afraid of causing other people trouble or embarrassing yourself, remember that most people not only don't mind catering to special diets and tastes, they are used to it. Almost everyone has prepared a special meal for a friend who is a vegetarian, lactose-intolerant, watching his or her weight, or allergic to fish. Most likely, they will be happy to do the same for you.

Eating at Restaurants

Depending on the diet you follow, even eating at restaurants with extensive menus to choose from can be difficult. It may take some time, but you will eventually learn which restaurants you can eat at and which you can't. This might mean abandoning some favorite spots and finding new ones, but usually you will find that there are options for eating out.

Try to frequent places that give you some choices, so that you are not always forced to order the same thing. If you don't see anything on the menu that you can eat, get creative. For instance, if the restaurant offers potatoes with entrées, but not as a separate menu item, ask your waiter if it's possible to get just a baked potato. Most restaurants will cater to individual needs as long as they have the ingredients in the kitchen and you don't ask for anything too fancy.

When you are with a group of people, you may not always feel comfortable suggesting restaurants that cater to your specific needs. Be flexible. Don't be afraid to try someplace new just because you are worried that it won't offer anything you can eat. You might suggest an alternative, however, if you know for sure that the restaurant your friends want to go to doesn't have anything for you. While you don't want to always be the deciding factor in where the group goes to eat, remember that your needs count, too.

Eating at School

Eating at school is not usually a big problem because you can bring your own food if necessary. However, if you are restricted to liquids, or are on TEN or TPN, you may feel self-conscious about not being able to eat more normal meals with your friends.

If you have already talked to your friends about IBD, you can simply tell them that you have to rest your stomach for a while. Some of them might be curious and ask more questions, but most will probably be satisfied with a brief explanation.

If you are not yet ready to discuss IBD with other people or don't want to call attention to yourself because you're not eating, be creative. Find a project that you can work on during lunchtime, such as helping a teacher in the classroom or studying for an upcoming test in the library. This will give you an excuse to be by yourself while others are eating lunch.

Remember, however, that you have no reason to be embarrassed, and you don't want to spend your life hiding out from other people. If you are honest with your friends, you will probably find that their curiosity fades quickly once they know what is happening. Before long, your lunches will seem completely normal.

Dealing with Other People

When you are diagnosed with Crohn's disease or ulcerative colitis, it affects your family and your friends. The people who are closest to you may experience a range of emotions, from fear to guilt to becoming suddenly overprotective or distant. Usually, they will adjust to the fact that you have a chronic illness, but it may take a while. In the meantime, it can help to know what to expect.

Handling Too Much Concern
One of the most common reactions people have to any chronic illness is to start focusing exclusively on your

health. Suddenly, people will ask, "How are you feeling?" instead of "What's going on?" or "How was your day?" While you probably recognize and appreciate their concern, you may also get tired of the constant questioning.

At a certain point, Monique's parents realized that they were asking Monique how she felt every time they saw her. "I'm sure it was really annoying," says her mom. "If people keep bugging you about how you feel, just ask them nicely to stop asking so much. Tell people that you want them to talk to you normally and to not always ask about your disease."

Sometimes, allowing people to help you will give them a positive way to focus their attention. Many people will ask you how you're feeling because they don't know how else to express their concern or support. If you can help them to feel useful in some way, they might feel more in control of the situation.

You may also find that people want to overprotect you. Your parents won't want you to overly exert yourself, and even friends might occasionally ask, "Are you sure you should do that?" When you are trying hard to feel as if nothing is wrong, this can be especially frustrating.

Acknowledge that people who feel protective of you are just concerned about your welfare, but (unless it comes from your doctor) don't feel obliged to follow advice if you don't agree with it. "You know best what your body can handle," says Dan. "And sometimes, even if it causes you a little discomfort, it's important to do something you really want to do. You occasionally have to indulge yourself a little bit. Just tell people you think you can handle it."

Coping with Resentment

Relationships might also become strained if other people start to resent that you are constantly in the spotlight. This often occurs with siblings. "I have a twin brother," says Darcy, "and we're not really that close. I feel like he's mad at me for getting so much of the attention when we were younger, because I was always sick."

Sometimes people fail to see the whole picture. If you feel that someone is jealous of your illness because it gets you attention, don't be shy about pointing out all the negatives to having a chronic disease. Usually, once they start to understand what you are going through, their resentment will vanish.

If you are worried that siblings are jealous of the attention you are receiving, talk to them about it. By acknowledging their feelings, you may be able to ease tensions. You might also explain that there are times when you are envious of them, such as when they are able to do things that you cannot. Speaking to your parents and asking them to spend additional time with your brothers or sisters may also help to resolve the problem.

Accepting People's Discomfort

Most people with IBD find that friends and family are extremely supportive and want to help as much as possible. However, there might be people in your life who seem to vanish or become more distant when they find out that you have IBD. There are several reasons for this.

Some people are uncomfortable with the idea of illness and simply do not know how to be around someone who is "sick." Occasionally, people get so worried or feel so helpless that they react by pulling away. Others may withdraw for reasons you will never know.

There are no simple answers for dealing with this, because everyone's situation is a little different. Sometimes, the most helpful thing you can do is to talk to the person and try to sort out the problem. Other times, it's best to give the person a little time to adjust to the fact that you have a chronic illness. Usually once he or she sees that you are still the same person, things will return to normal. If not, it is important to remember that their reaction means something about them, not about you.

Helping Others Adjust

Especially when you are first diagnosed, it may seem like all you can do is take care of yourself. There are so many emotional and physical adjustments for you to make that at first you might not consider that your family and friends are learning to cope with all of this, too.

If you suspect that your friends are feeling insecure or neglected because you have been spending less time with them, let them know that it is not a reflection on them. Even if you choose not to go into the details of IBD, explain that you may be less social than usual for a while, but that you still want to spend time with them. When you feel up to it, make an effort to initiate social activities.

Communicating honestly with your parents and demonstrating that you are capable of managing your care may help them from becoming overly anxious about your condition. Simple things such as taking your medications regularly and showing an interest in your health can go a long way in relieving your parents' concerns. If they feel that you are responsible enough to take care of yourself, they will probably be less protective.

Keeping a Positive Outlook

Maintaining a positive attitude may be the single most important factor in coping with Crohn's disease or ulcerative colitis. "You have to try not to concentrate on the negative things," says Darcy. "If you concentrate on the negative, you're only going to feel negative."

Although it may be hard when you are feeling sick, try to remember that your situation will eventually improve. Your flare-up will end. You will not feel awful every day of your life. You will find ways to deal with the day-to-day hassles. As Jessica says, "It's not all that bad. At least it's not something worse."

Probably, you will have times when you feel overwhelmed by IBD, when it seems to be taking over your life. During these times, remind yourself that IBD is only one part of who you are. You are not just someone with a chronic illness. You have interests, abilities, and opinions that have nothing to do with IBD. Concentrating on other things can help restore a sense of balance in your life. "You've got to focus on something that you enjoy," Dustin says. "The more you concentrate on being sick, the worse you're going to feel."

Glossary

abscess   An infected pocket of pus.

barium   A chalky-tasting substance used to highlight the digestive tract during X rays.

biologics   Medications made from the proteins, genes, and antibodies of living organisms.

chronic   Lasting a long time or recurring often.

colectomy   Surgical removal of the colon.

colon   The large intestine.

colonoscopy   A procedure to view the rectum and lower colon using a tiny camera attached to a long, narrow tube.

computerized tomography scan   An X ray procedure using a doughnut-shaped scanning machine; CT scan.

continent ileostomy   Surgical creation of a pouch inside the abdomen to collect waste; eliminates the need for an external bag following colectomy.

corticosteroids   Anti-inflammatory medications.

Crohn's colitis   Crohn's disease of the colon.

dysplasia   Abnormal cell patterns that can be an indication of cancer.

endoscopy   A procedure to examine the digestive tract using a tiny camera attached to a long, thin tube.

enema   A liquid inserted into the colon through the anus.

fistula   Abnormal channels leading from one section of intestine to another, or from the intestine to another organ.

flare-up   A period of active disease, when symptoms are present.

hemorrhaging   Heavy bleeding.

ileitis   Crohn's disease of the ileum.

ileoanal anastomosis   Surgical creation of a pouch that connects the small intestine and the anus; eliminates the need for an ostomy following a colectomy.

ileocolitis   Crohn's disease of the ileum and colon.

ileostomy   Surgical rerouting of waste through a hole in the abdominal wall; waste collects in a bag attached to the skin.

ileum   Lower part of the small intestine; attaches to the large intestine.

immunomodulators   Medications that help suppress the immune system.

J-pouch   See "ileoanal anastomosis."

kock pouch   See "continent ileostomy."

lactose-intolerance   Difficulty digesting milk products; results in diarrhea, cramping, and gas.

lower GI X rays   Barium X rays of the rectum and colon.

MRI   Magnetic resonance imaging; a procedure to obtain detailed pictures of internal organs using a magnetic field.

obstruction   A blockage in the intestines, caused by severe inflammation or scarring, that prevents the passage of intestinal contents.

osteoporosis   A decrease in bone density that can result in easily broken bones.

pan-ulcerative colitis   Ulcerative colitis of the rectum and colon.

perforation   A hole in the bowel wall that allows intestinal contents to escape.

pouchitis   An infection of the new pouch created during ileoanal anastomosis or continent ileostomy procedures; causes diarrhea, abdominal pain, and fever.

proctocolectomy   Surgical removal of the colon and rectum.

proctosigmoiditis   Ulcerative colitis of the rectum and lower colon.

remission   Period when a disease is inactive; when symptoms are not present.

resection   Surgical removal of diseased segments of the small intestine.

short-bowel syndrome   A condition that results when large amounts of small intestine have been removed and nutritional deficiencies arise.

sigmoidoscopy   A procedure to view the rectum and lower portion of the colon using a camera attached to a thin, narrow tube.

stoma   A surgically created hole in the abdominal wall; allows for the removal of waste following ileostomy.

stricture   A narrowed segment of intestine, usually caused by scarring from inflamed tissue.

strictureplasty   A procedure to widen segments of the bowel that have become too narrow.

TEN   Total enteral nutrition; the delivery of liquid nutrients through a tube into the stomach.

toxic megacolon   Severe inflammation of the colon that can lead to rupture.

TPN   Total parenteral nutrition; the delivery of liquid nutrients through a catheter into the bloodstream.

ulcerative proctitis   Ulcerative colitis of the rectum.

ultrasound   A procedure that uses sound waves to obtain pictures of internal organs.

upper GI X rays   Barium X rays of the esophagus, stomach, and small intestine.

Where to Go for Help

American Dietetic Association (ADA)
216 West Jackson Boulevard
Chicago, IL 60606-6995
(312) 899-0040
Consumer nutrition information line: (800) 360-1655
Web site: http://www.eatright.org
The ADA offers nutritional guidelines and assistance in locating registered dieticians.

American Gastroenterological Association
7910 Woodmont Avenue, 7th Floor
Bethesda, MD 20814
(301) 654-2055
Web site: http://www.gastro.org
This association offers information on IBD for patients and doctors. The Web site also features a message board and a physician locator to help identify gastroenterologists in your area.

Canadian Association of Gastroenterology
2902 South Sheridan Way
Oakville, ON Canada L65 7L6
(905) 829-2504 or (888) 780-0007
Web site: http://www.cag-acg.org
Compiles current research and information on digestive health.

Crohn's and Colitis Foundation of America (CCFA)
386 Park Avenue South, 17th Floor
New York, NY 10016-8804
(212) 685-3440 or (800) 932-2423
Web site: http://www.ccfa.org
The CCFA provides current information, news, research, and other support services for people with IBD. Check the Web site or call for information on local chapters.

Crohn's and Colitis Foundation of Canada
60 St. Clair Avenue East, Suite 600
Toronto, ON Canada M4T 1N5
(416) 920-5036 or (800) 387-1479
Web site: http://www.ccfc.ca
A great source for information, research, and support for people with IBD. Check the Web site or call for information on local chapters for more information.

Intestinal Disease Foundation
Landmarks Building, Suite 525
Pittsburgh, PA 15219-1138
(412) 261-5888 or (877) 587-9606
Web site: http://www.intestinalfoundation.org
Offers online information and a subscription newsletter for people with Crohn's disease, ulcerative colitis, and IBS.

National Digestive Diseases Information Clearinghouse
2 Information Way
Bethesda, MD 20892-3570
(301) 654-3810 or (800) 891-5389
Web site: http://www.niddk.nih.gov/health/digest/nddic.htm

Provides information on digestive health and clinical trials online and by phone.

North American Society for Pediatric Gastroenterology,
     Hepatology, and Nutrition
P.O. Box 6
Flourtown, PA 19031
(215) 233-0808
Web site: http://www.naspgn.org
This Web site has information on IBD and related conditions; it also features a search function to help locate pediatric gastroenterologists in your area.

Pediatric Crohn's and Colitis Association
P.O. Box 188
Newton, MA 0218-0002
(617) 290-0902
Web site: http://pcca.hypermart.net
Packed with information on IBD in children and teens, this Web site includes articles on growth problems and advocacy in schools.

Ostomy Support

United Ostomy Association, Inc.
19772 MacArthur Boulevard, Suite 200
Irvine, CA 92612-2405
(800) 826-0826
Web site: http://www.uoa.org
A source for information, resources, and support for people who have had ostomy surgery.

United Ostomy Association of Canada, Inc.
P.O. Box 825-50 Charles Street East
Toronto, ON Canada M4Y 2NY
(416) 595-5452 or (888) 969-9698
Web site: http://www.ostomycanada.ca
Contact this organization for information, resources, and
support for people who have had ostomy surgery.

Pain Management

American Chronic Pain Association
P.O. Box 850
Rocklin, CA 95677
(916) 632-0922
Web site: http://theacpa.org
Offers support and coping strategies for people managing
chronic pain.

Surgery

American College of Surgeons
633 North St. Clair Street
Chicago, IL 60611
(312) 202-5000
Web site: http://www.facs.org
Provides information on different types of surgery and on
choosing the right doctor.

American Society of Colon and Rectal Surgeons
85 West Algonquin Road, Suite 550
Arlington Heights, IL 60005
(847) 290-9184
Web site: http://www.fascrs.org
Look at these online brochures for information about complications of IBD and the surgical procedures to correct them.

Society of Laproendoscopic Surgeons
7330 Southwest 62nd Place, Suite 410
Miami, FL 33143
(800) 446-2659
Web site: http://www.sls.org
This Web site offers information on laparoscopic and endoscopic surgery and enables you to search for a laparoscopic or endoscopic surgeon in your area.

Web Sites

Due to the changing nature of Internet links, the Rosen Publishing Group, Inc., has developed an online list of Web sites related to the subject of this book. This site is updated regularly. Please use this link to access the list:

http://www.rosenlinks.com/cop/crdc

For Further Reading

Cash, Thomas F. *The Body Image Workbook: An 8-Step Program for Learning to Like Your Looks.* Oakland, CA: New Harbinger Publications, 1997.

Donoghue, Paul J. *Sick and Tired of Feeling Sick and Tired: Living with Invisible Chronic Illness.* New York: W. W. Norton, 2000.

Gomez, Joan. *Positive Options for Crohn's Disease: Self-Help and Treatment.* Alameda, CA: Hunter House, 2000.

Reinhard, Tonia. *Gastrointestinal Disorders and Nutrition.* Chicago: Contemporary Books, 2002.

Saibil, Fred. *Crohn's Disease and Ulcerative Colitis: Everything You Need to Know.* Buffalo, NY: Firefly Books, 1997.

Scala, James. *The New Eating Right for a Bad Gut: The Complete Nutritional Guide to Ileitis, Colitis, Crohn's Disease, and Inflammatory Bowel Disease.* New York: Plume, 2000.

Sklar, Jill. *The First Year: Crohn's Disease and Ulcerative Colitis.* New York: Marlowe & Company, 2002.

Stein, Stanley H., and Richard P. Rood, eds. *Inflammatory Bowel Disease: A Guide for Patients and Their Families.* Philadelphia, PA: Lippincott, Williams, and Wilkins, 1998.

Steiner-Grossman, Penny. *The New People Not Patients: A Source Book for Living with Inflammatory Bowel Disease*. New York: The Crohn's and Colitis Foundation of America, 1997.

Trachter, Amy. *Coping with Crohn's Disease: Manage Your Physical Symptoms and Overcome the Emotional Challenges*. Oakland, CA: New Harbinger Publications, 2001.

Zonderman, Jon. *Understanding Crohn's Disease and Ulcerative Colitis*. Jackson, MS: University Press of Mississippi, 2000.

Zukerman, Eugenia, and Julie R. Ingelfinger. *Coping with Prednisone (and Other Cortisone-Related Medicines)*. New York: St. Martin's Press, 1998.

Bibliography

Bolen, Barbara Bradley, Ph.D., and W. Grant Thompson. *Breaking the Bonds of Irritable Bowel Syndrome: A Psychological Approach to Regaining Control of Your Life.* Oakland, CA: New Harbinger Publications, 2000.

Donoghue, Paul J. *Sick and Tired of Feeling Sick and Tired: Living with Invisible Chronic Illness.* New York: W. W. Norton, 2000.

Kalibjian, Cliff. *Straight from the Gut: Living with Crohn's Disease and Ulcerative Colitis.* Sebastopol, CA: O'Reilly and Co., 2003.

Salt, William B., III, and Neil F. Neimark. *Irritable Bowel Syndrome and the Mind Body Spirit Connection: 7 Steps for Living a Healthy Life with a Functional Bowel Disorder, Crohn's Disease or Colitis.* Columbus, OH: Parkview Publishing, 2002.

Scala, James. *The New Eating Right for a Bad Gut: The Complete Nutritional Guide to Ileitis, Colitis, Crohn's Disease, and Inflammatory Bowel Disease.* New York: Plume, 2000.

Sklar, Jill. *The First Year: Crohn's Disease and Ulcerative Colitis.* New York: Marlowe & Company, 2002.

Stein, Stanley H., and Richard P. Rood, eds. *Inflammatory Bowel Disease: A Guide for Patients and Their Families.* Philadelphia, PA: Lippincott, Williams, and Wilkins, 1998.

Index

A
abdominal pain/cramping, 14, 15, 17, 20, 27, 29, 30, 32, 53
abscess, 17, 21, 32, 33, 47, 48, 49
addiction, 44–46
allergic reactions, 41, 43, 44
anal muscles, 52, 53, 54
antibiotics, 42, 53, 58
antidiarrheals, 44, 84
anti-inflammatory medicines, 6, 36–40, 41
anus, 10, 52, 53
appetite, increased, 6, 38, 39
appetite loss, 14, 42, 60
arthritis, 18–19
Asacol, 38
azathioprine (Imuran), 40, 41

B
barium enema, 25, 27–28
bathroom trips, 73, 83–84
biologics, 42–44
biopsies, 10, 29, 31
body image, 78–79
bone density problems, 6, 19
bowel channel, narrowing of, 10
bowel movements, constant need for, 14, 52
bowel perforation, 17, 47, 48, 51

bowel prep, 27, 31, 58
breathing difficulties, 44

C
camps for children with IBD, 7, 78
cancer, 19–20, 47
  colon, 19–20, 51
  rectal, 53
celiac disease (gluten intolerance), 5, 6
chronic illness, 6, 7, 9, 10, 21, 45, 71, 77, 79, 90, 92, 93, 94
ciprofloxacin (Cipro), 42
Colazal, 38
colectomy, 51–52, 56
colon, 10, 11, 12, 17, 20, 27, 29, 30, 31, 38, 42, 46, 51, 52, 53, 54
colonoscopy, 5, 6, 20, 28, 30–32, 77
computerized/computed tomography scan (CT or CAT), 32
constipation/constipated, 5
corticosteroids, 19, 38–40, 43, 58, 78
counseling, 76, 79
Crohn, Dr. Burrill B., 10
Crohn's and Colitis Foundation of America (CCFA), 7, 12, 13, 49, 50, 76, 77, 78

About the Author

Christina Potter, an educator, lives in San Diego, California. Her husband and a close friend both have Crohn's disease.

Acknowledgments

This book was a group effort. I could not have written it without help from the following people: Coby, Dan, Daniel, Darcy, Dustin, Jessica, Monique, and Sue, who spoke candidly with me about the details of living with Crohn's disease and ulcerative colitis; Kathy Dalecio, who tirelessly helped me establish contacts, even in the middle of her summer vacation; Dr. Fiona Vajk, who provided coping suggestions and proofreading assistance; and Jill Jarnow, who offered me the project in the first place.

Editor: Jill Jarnow